The Art
of the Myth

Maine Essays

ISBNs: 979-8-9915327-1-6 (hardcover); 979-8-9915327-0-9 (paperback); 979-8-9915327-2-3 (ebook)

Published 2024 by Alameda Editions
Cover design by Molly Mortimer, Mayfly book design
Cover photo by Viktoriya @torirori, unsplash.com
Interior design by Molly Mortimer, Mayfly book design
The text of this book is set in FreightText Pro

First Edition

The Tyrone Guthrie Centre in Annaghmakerrig, Ireland provided time and atmosphere for the editing and cobbling together of this collection, over several Residencies.

Grants from the Colby College Humanities Division supported the writing of several of the works in this collection, and are here gratefully acknowledged.

These pieces originally appeared, some in slightly different form, in *New England Monthly, Down East, Yankee, Maine Décor, Architecture Boston,* or *Route 9.* "Effort" and "The Northwoods Balladeer" were previously unpublished.

Library of Congress Catalog Number: 2024919089

Library of Congress Cataloging-in-Publication Data
Burke, Michael D., 1953-
The Art of the Myth/Michael D. Burke

Michael D. Burke

The Art
of the
Myth

Maine Essays

Alameda Editions

Also by Michael D. Burke

The Same River Twice: A Boatman's Journey Home
Maine's Place in the Environmental Imagination (editor)

For the students, and their patience

"I thought that telling stories was the only conceivable occupation for a superfluous person such as myself."

Bruce Chatwin, "I Always Wanted to Go to Patagonia"

Contents

Foreword

I didn't set out as a writer to write about Maine, or to write as much as I have about Maine. But there might have been an inevitability about the choice of subject: I was in western Massachusetts when I began taking up Maine as my topic, and having spent considerable time in wilderness areas of the American West and Alaska, Maine was the closest thing to those landscapes and spaces available to me. In short, finding myself in New England in the early 1908s I was drawn to the state among those six with the most open spaces.

Then in 1987 we moved to Maine; "we," the woman who would become my wife, two kids, a dog. There's another story in that "we," but suddenly I was no longer a visitor, a tourist, a dabbler. Now I was inside. Not a "Mainer"—I'll never be a Mainer, according to the logic of Maine—but at least I couldn't be accused of being From Away anymore. My license plate gave me legitimacy, and I started to absorb the kind of knowledge that a local does.

I think I wanted to explain Maine to myself, and I did so by writing about it. Such explanations are only partial, and filtered through all kinds of assumptions, beliefs, privileges. My particular subjects included the rural, the wild, and, as much as possible, the interior of the state, not the coast, which seemed to me to be well-documented enough as is. I was fortunate to have the late, great magazine, *New England Monthly*, as my home for a short time; it had an impressive group of writers and editors during its brief life, and the magazine provided me a forum in which to indulge my interests.

I would like to have written more on groups of people in the state, on Somali immigrants, indigenous communities; on rural poverty and struggling villages. Some of the latter have found their way in here, but for better or worse I made my claim on the rural and on individuals, on the quirky and yet what to me felt characteristic, at least of a certain slice of the state. A different writer will have to address what has been left out.

The collection is in four sections, commencing with experiences I had with experts doing odd things. Next are experiences I had more or less on my own, also doing odd things. A third section takes up subjects that captured my attention, where the subject is in the foreground rather than my experience. Finally, there are the longest piece in the collection and the shortest, which in some peculiar way pair.

Since the first piece was written we've been through three impeachments, 9/11, the Great Recession, the Covid-19 pandemic, a recognition of how fragile democracy is, and the on-going crisis of climate change. None of that shows up here: One wouldn't come to these stories for their timeliness, their currency, for breaking news; one would turn to them to understand what it was like to attend a church service deep in the Maine woods, forage for fiddlehead ferns, sleep in a tent in the middle of winter, deal with a fallen maple, or immerse yourself in a season of county fairs.

One

Some People Know What They're Doing

The pieces in this section range from Maine Game Wardens to playing trombone in a small town's summer Park Band. The first essay, "Moose Patrol," sets the tone for the stories I am most drawn to: unusual occupations and unusual people, subjects which gives me the pleasure of unpacking those oddities for the reader. The rest share that theme, with whitewater guides, maple syrup makers, pictograph fanatics, fiddleheaders, and lobsterers as topics. And trombones.

These appeared in *New England Monthly* or *Down East Magazine*, between 1987 and 2018. Only "Effort" was previously unpublished.

Moose Patrol
(1987)

6:45 a.m., fifteen minutes before sunrise. In other parts of New England it is the dawning of a Sunday at the very height of leaf— and World Series—season. Pumpkins are scattered brightly across the fields, and for someone somewhere, a distant honking overheard becomes a V of Canada geese wisely headed south.

The potential pleasures of a mid-October New England morning are lost on Warden Bruce Farrar, Warden Specialist Peter McPheters, and me. We are hidden in a swale of dried leaves and moss in northwestern Maine, a few miles north of the 46th parallel and 250 yards east of the Canadian border, watching an almost invisible trail that winds through a stand of cedar and spruce. McPheters is wrapped tightly in a wool blanket. Farrar is sitting on his jacket, engrossed in a detective novel. I am shivering.

Soon a thin sun appears, generating a weak light but no heat through the spindly trees. The temperature has risen to a few degrees above freezing since we left the Warden Service cabin near St. Cyprien, Quebec, at four a.m. We talk, when we talk, in whispers, and our movement is limited to quietly shifting shoulders, hips, and buttocks from one uncomfortable position to another. I take some solace in noticing that McPheters and Farrar aren't immune to the cold either: McPheter's boots, sticking out from under his blanket, tremble, and Farrar's book shakes in his hand. Yet they seem to find nothing remarkable about sitting perfectly still in the Maine woods, shivering like mad.

"What's the longest you might stay out here?" I whisper, hoping to hear that they can't possibly intend to remain beyond noon. "All night, sometimes," Farrar answers dryly, and a new round of uncontrollable shivering seizes me. "Takes patience to be a warden," he adds, and I silently note that it takes a great deal more than that. An abnormal stubbornness and an extra layer of fat would be handy assets as well.

The three of us—along with Sergeant Patrick Dorian and Warden Richard Stone, hidden on the other side of the trail not far away—are here for the second day of moose hunting season in Quebec. In the Warden Service this is known as boundary patrol, an annual event in which two dozen wardens try to outwit hundreds of Canadian moose hunters stretched along roughly two hundred miles of the border between Maine and Quebec.

From the air, the border in this area looks like a punk haircut, shaved on one side, thick growth on the other. Except for the occasional clear-cut, lake, or dirt road, northern Maine is one big woods extending right to the border, where the forest has been cleared away and farmlands and small towns begin. The Maine side is perfect moose habitat: bogs, tender young trees, few people, and plenty of company (the Maine moose herd north of the Canadian Pacific Railroad line, which bisects the state, is estimated at eighteen thousand to twenty-three thousand head). The Canadian side, on the other hand, offers almost nothing of interest to the average moose. So when moose season opens in Quebec, hundreds of Canadians in fluorescent orange caps and vests drive to the border in their pickups and four-wheel-drives and do one of three things: they wait for a wandering moose to stray onto the border and then shoot it; they hide themselves in tree seats (some as elaborate as small cabins) and use moose calls to entice the moose across, then shoot it; or they take a short stroll into Maine and shoot it here. The first two strategies are legal; the third is common, according to the wardens, and it is poaching.

In terms of public image, the Maine Game Warden sits comfortably somewhere between the Canadian Mountie and Daniel Boone. The citizens of Maine expect wardens to be backwoods *savants*, have an ability to solve any problem in the forest, be as rugged as bark; for the most part wardens deliver. Boundary patrol is like other traditional warden duties: it requires an ability to track and understand the habits of animals and men, to orient oneself through a trail-less woods, and to wait for hour after hour in the worst conditions imaginable. But those skills are used less often now, as the character of the Warden Service changes to reflect the changes in Maine itself. The modern warden's duties begin with fish and game, but is also asked to enforce regulations pertaining to all-terrain vehicles and snowmobiles, to monitor the white-water rafting industry, to perform searches and rescues, and, while he or she is at it, to enforce all state laws. There are even duties one could never predict.

"For some reason, the woods are a popular place for people to kill themselves," says Lieutenant Steve Hall, a warden at Greenville Regional Headquarters on Moosehead Lake. "Someone will pull off the road a bit and walk off and do it, and we're usually the ones who find them." North of the Canadian Pacific Railroad line, in an 11,400-quare-mile area that has no other law-enforcement personnel, wardens are often the first to investigate accidents and crimes committed in or out of the woods. Thus, they confront such non-wildlife problems as plane wrecks, drug busts, asphyxiations (when someone in a camper or cabin burns up all the oxygen inside while trying to heat it), plus the occasional suicide, and mount search and rescue patrols, most of which seem to occur in terrible weather. "I've sent people out in blinding snowstorms on snowmobiles," says Hall, "when it's hard to see thin ice on lakes and ponds that the snowmobile will break through. And it's not uncommon to have to hike these mountains at night."

Given the demands and outright dangers of warden service, I muse, would anyone in his right mind want the job? "I don't order these people to do these things," says Hall. "They do them on their own. It's not a job for them. If it was a job, you couldn't get anyone to do it. It's a profession." It's also an exclusive profession: there are only 126 district wardens covering a state of 31,867 square miles, just 150 square miles less than the area of the other five New England States combined. And some of those professionals are lucky enough to draw boundary patrol duty in moose season.

Early Saturday morning, Warden Pilot Dana Toothaker and I are aloft in his Cessna 185, in search of orange hats. We are flying the boundary north from Sandy Bay to Big Ten township, advising warden patrols on the ground where to look for poachers, picking out trails into Maine, and hoping to spot a fluorescent-topped Canadian bobbing along on the wrong side of the line.

If the abrupt way the woods end didn't give the border away, the number of cars along the Canadian side surely would. From the air, we can see groups of hunters standing by the cars and strolling along the edge of the woods. Toothaker points out some tree seats, all facing the border. Over the St. John River, he banks the plane to take a closer look at the latest change in the landscape: rocks tossed into the river to form a bridge poachers can easily walk across. Farther along there is a wire pulley strung across the river so hunters can pull a telltale canoe back to Quebec after they've landed their colleagues in Maine.

On the St. John we see several parties in canoes. A pair of wardens, Charlie Davis and Mike Favreau, are disguised as hunters in a boat upstream of the others. Toothaker directs them by radio to where several canoes appear to have pulled over, perhaps poised to make the move into Maine. Later I learned that as the wardens rounded a bend in the river and came within sight of the canoes, one of the hunters pointed his rifle at them, using the scope to check them out. How could he tell, I asked Davis, whether the man was studying him or taking aim? Davis is a bear of a man, with bushy eyebrows and a shy manner. He shrugged. "Oh, well now," he said, looking embarrassed to admit his faith in human nature, "I don't think they'd be doing that."

I was to have met Sergeant Pat Dorian late that morning, but he and his patrol were busy watching a hat—all they could see of a poacher—moving down a trail that joined the one they were hiding beside. They didn't move in; they hoped the hat would decide the area was safe and come back the next day with others. Besides, a move might have meant a footrace to the border, and wardens don't always win. At any rate, the delay caused by Dorian's stakeout meant that I would have to endure four and a half hours in the Cessna roller coaster before Toothaker set down and mercifully released me.

Pat Dorian is a bulldog. One imagines the thirty-six-year-old warden would be unpleasant to tangle with, less because he is physically intimidating than because it's clear that he wouldn't let go, that in his tenacious way he would pursue an issue to its conclusion, mentally, legally, or physically. I met up with Dorian and three others—McPheters, Farrar, and Stone—at Dole Pond, where Toothaker finally landed his plane. From the pond, the five of us split up into two trucks and headed back to the warden camp. Along the way a call comes in to Dorian from Toothaker: one of the patrols Toothaker has been directing from the air has pinched a hunter inside Maine. A warden has radioed for advice on what the charge should be—hunting without a license (a $284 fine) or killing a moose without a permit (mandatory $1,000 fine, three days in jail, and possible loss of weapon). Has the man been asked what he was doing in Maine with a rifle? asks Dorian. The reply comes back: "The guy says he was hunting moose." Dorian and McPheters break into laughter. "Then

I think you can get him for moose hunting without a license," Dorian says.

McPheters, who is forty, is a compact man of medium height who wears a thick black moustache, smokes a pipe, and is an expert in the art of using a moose call—a two pound coffee can with one end cut off, a hole punched in the other end, and a shoestring knotted through it. By manipulating a wet shoestring, an adept can produce mournful, moose-y tones all day long. To demonstrate, McPheters composes himself and arranges the can under his arm like a concertmaster settling a violin under his chin. He lifts his head and loses himself in the first, serene note of his song—a honking, bleating imitation of a moose's love cry.

Back at warden camp, a three-room cabin by a small pond, the wardens settle at the kitchen table, drinking beer and swapping stories in the fading hours of afternoon. After a dinner of steamed clams and the pork and beans that Dorian's wife sent from Greenville, most of the wardens decide—despite having arisen at three that morning and facing the same schedule tomorrow—that they'll make a run across the border to a bar in St. Camille and try to catch the first game of the World Series.

The El Centro is packed with Canadian moose hunters. There had been dark talk among the wardens of wild nights here, but the place is subdued when we enter. To me, it seems odd for the wardens to venture into a bar frequented by the very people they've spent the day trying to catch, but McPheters shrugs it off. "I don't think they resent it when we pop them. They know they're taking a chance by poaching. For the most part they're pretty good fellows." Once, he remembers, he and another warden walked into the El Centro and saw two hunters they had once arrested. "They came over and bought us drinks," he says.

The Series game isn't available on the bar's wide-screen television, which leaves us to watch one of several hockey games or be entertained by the unexpected appearance of two dancers—the exotic variety, at least as the species is construed in Quebec—on the bar's tiny stage. While one of the dancers weaves her spell in high heels, white ankle socks, and a tight white bathing suit, I try to converse with Mike Favreau ("I always resented that I missed out on Vietnam") and Charlie Davis ("See that big guy in the corner? I bet he pays one of those girls to come over and dance on his table") over the roar of the disco music. After a self-imposed limit of two beers apiece, we leave at the respectable hour of ten and return to camp.

As promised, we rise at three. There's little conversation as the wardens move about, heating up leftover beans, chewing on grocery-store doughnuts, trying to get the coffee brewer to work. Having learned from experience on yesterday's ambush, they pack extra long underwear and jackets, and Dick Stone brings a thermos of coffee. Each warden stuffs sandwiches and potato chips in his knapsack, and we leave.

I ride in Stone and Farrar's truck on the dark, rutted road into Quebec, then back into Maine, to the site of the previous day's patrol. By five we've arrived at a slash pile, where our hike will begin. The stars and a bit of moon give some light, but not much. The wardens string out ahead through the woods. Stone, who is twenty-seven and very quiet, waits for me and politely takes the last position in line.

On the way out after their patrol yesterday, Dorian and the others had marked a trail with red plastic flagging, as though marking trees for cutting. When they'd run out of flags, they made blazes with their knives, small marks that a poacher might not see and that are hard for us to find in the dark. When we lose the blazes, we stop and shine our lights along the trees until the next one is found. We make our way up the slope of one ridge, stepping over logs and downed limbs and snags. The ground, soft from rains, causes many stumbles and slips, and every spruce seems to have a branch at forehead level.

At the first trace of dawn, the gloom lessens and the trees take on a shadowy reality. We stop at a tiny creek to get a drink, then hike over the last ridge and into the bog where the poacher trails are. Less than a half mile from the border now, we come to the trail (if trail it is; it's almost impossible to distinguish from the surrounding vegetation, and when we're not standing on it I can't find it). The path splits here, one branch heading north, the other northeast. The wardens decide on the northeast trail, and the ambush is planned: McPheters, Farrar, and I will go up the trail fifty yards, move up the slope to the right, and hide. Dorian and Stone will stay where they are and hide on the other side. Each group has a portable radio; when someone comes down the trail Farrar will hit the call button twice to alert the others, then close in from behind before the poacher passes Dorian. "It's expected that he'll run," Farrar says. "He knows that if he gets to the border we can't touch him," adds Dorian, "but if we can lay hands on him before then . . ." He smiles his bulldog smile.

We hustle up to our places and arrange ourselves. It is six-thirty, and the wardens have scheduled it perfectly. By the time we finish wrapping ourselves up for the wait, it'll be just about sunrise, when the shooting will start. Farrar pulls out an extra jacket to sit on and takes out his paperback. McPheters pulls his red-and-black-checked blanket around himself. I fall asleep for a minute and begin to snore. McPheters nudges me with his boot. I eat a bit of the lunch I brought, hoping it will stoke some internal fires. Then I swaddle myself tighter into a heavy wool blanket, replace my baseball cap with a polypropylene hat, put on some gloves, and try to convince myself that I am indeed warming up.

Within half an hour I am shivering furiously, great spasms passing through my body. Shortly after dawn, the first distant shots are fired. Gradually they come closer, booming louder although still sporadic: a shot, then in fifteen minutes another.

One sounds closer than the others, and it occurs to me that we are hidden in the woods where men with high-powered rifles are sneaking around, looking for something large and brown to kill. Suddenly I feel large. At every shot I tense, expecting action, but Farrar continues reading. "Someone's bored," is all he says.

Toothaker's plane flies the border again this morning to direct other patrols. Farrar switches on his radio and whispers to the pilot to see if he knows who won the Series game last night. Nothing comes back but static. After another hour the wardens adopt a more aggressive tactic: they will use the moose call, hoping to trick a poacher into showing himself. Dorian has the call at his hiding place. A few tentative squawks sound through the forest. McPheters, the virtuoso, cringes.

Then the shots stop altogether. At ten, after three and a half hours, Dorian comes over to our spot, bundled in his camouflage fatigues. "Hot, dry, and dusty, eh?" Farrar says to him. "Jesus Christ," Dorian growls. I jump up and begin stomping the ground, trying to force blood into my fingers and toes; meanwhile the wardens talk it over and agree that their man isn't coming down his trail today, and so, after all the preparation, all the sitting, all the waiting, all the cold, we break the ambush.

By the time we reach the trucks it's almost one—ten hours since the wardens got up, and still about nine hours before any of them will get to their homes. Nevertheless, on the drive back to camp they stop to investigate a truck parked in a clear-cut. It might, they say, belong to a suicide, or someone fishing a closed pond, or a beaver trapper setting his traps too early, or a moose hunter jumping the Maine season. Only after an hour and a half of poking around—surveying the pond with binoculars, walking to a camping area on the other side, warning me to take off my blue and white cap because a hunter might mistake it for the rump of a white-tailed deer, inspecting the parked truck for signs of what its owner might be doing, and changing a flat on one of their own trucks—only then are the wardens ready to leave.

The next morning I go down to Greenville Warden Service headquarters to witness the results of the first day of the Maine season, which opened half an hour before sunrise. By the time I arrive, at nine-thirty, the first two moose have already been brought in.

When a moose is killed it has to be taken to one of the state's nine tagging stations, where it will be weighed (the biggest I saw was 980 pounds, field-dressed; add another fifth of that for the live weight), measured, and its age determined. The hunter must present his permit and explain where he shot it; every hunter is assigned a zone, and it is as illegal to shoot a moose outside your zone as it is to shoot without a permit. Permits are distributed by lottery in Maine; in 1986 52,919 people applied for the 900 resident permits issued. By noon, forty-one moose have been tagged, and about ninety are expected by day's end.

Later in the morning, Pat Dorian arrived for a quick lunch. There's a moose in the back of his pickup. He is just stopping in, having been on patrol since five. His cargo is a carcass he confiscated from some hunters who had shot it outside their zone. Worse than that, they had lied when he encountered them. "We stopped to check their permit," Dorian says, "and we got to talking, and this guy asks if I know a place where he can wash his hands. We ask them where they shot the moose and they say they got it down on the West Branch of the Penobscot. I ask them if they put in at Hannibal's Crossing and they say yeah, they did. So we go on our way and I say to Roger, 'Does it make any sense to you that a guy would be looking for water to wash his hands when he just got done taking a moose out of a river?' We drive like hell over to Hannibal's Crossing to take a look. The bank is all dirt, and there's no sign of anyone dragging anything up the bank. So then we go chasing after these guys, catch up to them at the Greenville turnoff from the Golden Road. They said they were going to Greenville, but they were on their way to Millinocket."

It took some doing, the piecing together of contradictory statements and an unwillingness to give up until he got the right answers, but eventually Dorian caught the hunters in their lie. Then, having pursued this particular issue to its conclusion, the bulldog took their moose.

Thirty Thousand Holes

(2001)

When maple season began early last March, my youngest daughter and I headed out to our tiny sugarbush for the ritual tapping of the trees. She carried the tapping drill and I carried the six buckets, and I made a trail on snowshoes that she followed. At the trees I drilled the holes then hammered in the spiles, and she hung the buckets on the spiles. The final part of the ritual was when she held her finger under the spile to taste the first few sweet drops.

"Listen," I said.

She stopped and held her breath. We could hear the slow ping, ping, ping of the sap falling drop by drop into the empty bucket—a high, sweet, musical sound.

A few weeks later I was at Jean-Claude Paré's remote sugarhouse on Dole Pond in Somerset County, off the Golden Road and a few miles from the border with Quebec, his home. There was no pinging, but a roar; no buckets, but miles of tubing; no bit-and-brace drills, but an array of huge, steaming, gleaming equipment, Rube Goldberg-esque in its complexity.

Jean-Claude is one of the 45 or so large-scale sugarers operating in two clusters along the northwest border of Maine and Quebec: one cluster is the Golden Road camps, and the other, slightly further north, the St. Aurelie camps. The quaint image of the down-state sugarmaker who taps a few hundred of his trees to supplement his farm income, using oxen and sleds to haul the sap, doesn't capture the reality of the Somerset County sugarers. This is industrial sugaring, with sugarbushes ranging in size from 8,000 to 80,000 taps. However, "industrial" is not the same as "profitable": Most of these men aspire to make their living from maple, but few do. One of those who might someday is Jean-Claude Paré.

Like most agricultural occupations, sugaring is fraught with threats and crises, though sugaring seems to have more than its fair share. In '98 the legendary Ice Storm damaged many sugarbushes when the maples lost their crowns, bent and broken under the load of ice. The weather is the great variable of course: some years are too warm and the sap runs fast for a few days then stops; or too cold, so the sap hardly runs at all. Then there are bears and squirrels, moose too. The bear will rip at the tubing, the moose will walk through a sugarbush strung with tubing, inadvertently getting tangled in the lines; squirrels may be the most persistent problem, scurrying back and forth between their homes in the trees and the neighborhood sweet shop— the tubing closest to the trees.

For the Somerset County camps there is also the problem of the tenuous possession of their trees, or, rather, the holes in the trees: the sugarers are almost all working on leased land, and what they lease is only the right to tap the trees. The leases are granted by the big wood-products companies which own much of the North Woods; for many years that was International Paper and Great Northern Paper. But in 1999 the North Woods were going through a churning turnover, and it is sometimes difficult to know who owns what anymore. In fact, Jean-Claude didn't know who owned his land, though he knew the land was managed for the owners by Wagner Forest Management. Like most other sugarers, his lease on the taps runs only year to year, yet he has several hundred thousand dollars invested in his operation and he is not a wealthy man: before he began sugaring he worked in a factory in Quebec, making jeans. Because he is Canadian with a business in the U.S., he has to secure his (Canadian) bank loans with his personal property: his house, in other words. He is mortgaged to the limit, and it is all at risk, every season. Given all the turnover in land ownership and the uncertainties of sugaring, how can he justify the investment? He shrugs. "It is for that I worry," he says with a smile, in his slightly fractured but entirely workable English.

Indeed, Jean-Claude seems unaffected by all of these worries. He is a portly, friendly fellow, 42 years old. His portliness is deceiving: I followed him for two days as he bounded from place to place, nimbly leapt onto platforms, raced up a snow-covered hill on snowshoes while I labored to keep up. Jean-Claude works long hours, in difficult conditions, with all manner of problems hovering around him from a variety of sources, and he beams: he is the happiest man I've met in years.

The threats to his livelihood are made real when I turn off the Golden Road towards Dole Pond on a sunny day. The two mile road is a muddy sluice, littered with downed trees and timber-cutting equipment. To make my way around a huge metal dinosaur, a slasher, I wait while the operator lifts two of the foot pads out of the way, and swings the whizzing circular saw above the roof of my vehicle, then I inch past. This woods crew is cutting the lot next to Jean-Claude's, and the symbolism is acute, though Jean-Claude doesn't seem too worried. He has talked to the regional forester, Steve Wieder, who assures him (and me, when I call) that there are no plans to cut Jean-Claude's trees, and reminds me that some of these camps have been going for 50 years or more under the same year-by-year policy.

When I arrive, Jean-Claude is just pulling up from the left of the two muddy roads in the sugarbush that make a V ending at his camp and sugarhouse. He proudly shows me the operation, including the boiling room, which used to be the garage of a lumber camp when Jean-Claude bought it. It is painted a garish combination of green, red, and blue. "The paint was to sale?" Jean-Claude explains. He set up this sugarbush in 1996 with 16,000 taps, after first sugaring in 1990 in a different location on the Golden Road. Now he has 30,000 taps.

We drive up the right hand side of the V. At the end of the short road is a pump house, roaring because of the diesel generator that runs all day during the season. We hop out and check on the generator, leaving Jean-Claude's truck running, which is the pace at which he does everything during the season: preparing for the next thing while attending to this one.

Later we take a walk on snowshoes through the other side of the bush. The snow has become so soft in mid-March that even on snowshoes we punch through. The hill is not steep, but I try to imagine carrying 20 to 30 pounds of gear in a pack on snowshoes, up the hill, working all day long.

Which is what Jean-Claude and his crew of family (four children and his wife) and three hired hands do. Loaded with gas-powered tapping drills, wires, spiles, spools of tubing, they spread out one day in February and start the long process of tapping. Last year it took three and a half weeks to place the 30,000 taps. At most they could get 2200 taps drilled per day; the year before they were able to set only 800 taps each day because of the weather. While Jean-Claude is telling me this I do the math: If a crew of nine puts in 2200 taps in an eight-hour day, the crew is placing one tap every two minutes, which seems very fast.

The taps are at the beginning of a 5/16″ line of plastic tubing, which is itself connected to a larger, lateral line which then feeds into a mainline, a heavy black tube of one-inch PVC that runs straight down the hill to one of the two pump houses. The mainlines can each take up to 400 of the feeder lines; Jean-Claude has 28 mainlines on the left side of the V and 71 on the right. In these large sugarbushes, gravity is a friend, but not enough of one: the generator at each pump house keeps a vacuum going, pulling the sap down the hill. The mainlines end at a chamber in the pump house, where the sap enters, fills, then is released with a whoosh and a splash into the holding tank, a 1000 gallon stainless steel basin like a huge bathtub. From there the sap is pumped down hill to the sugarhouse.

"See the circle?" Jean-Claude says in his lilting accent, pointing at the base of a tree. The snow has melted away from the tree, where a bit of bare ground shows through. "Some say this means it is good for the sap, yes? Some say it is bad," Jean-Claude adds with a shrug. "It is for this I don't know if we are to have a good year or not so good year."

We walk further up the slope, until we come to a tiny, disintegrating log cabin sunk into the snow, with a wooden chair out front. The cabin belonged to the man who used to work this bush, more than 25 years before. Jean-Claude met him a few years ago. The man told Jean-Claude he used buckets and spiles, and a team of horses, to gather the sap. We stand there, marveling at how hard that kind of work must have been. Further on we come to a beech tree. "We say, in the past, a beech tree in the bush means the bush is bad. Now we say it is good," says Jean-Claude. He shrugs again: just another example of the mysteries of sugaring.

I hear a whistling somewhere nearby. "What's that?" I ask. Jean-Claude looks around until he spots it, then scuttles over on the snowshoes to a line and holds it up. The tap has come loose from its hole, and so the suction from the vacuum down the hill is pulling air through it, hence the whistle. We come across such whistlers regularly, and having brought no tools, use tree branches to pound them back into place.

We return to the sugarcamp for lunch, then go next door to the boiling room. It is in the boiling room where the sugaring operation gets most complicated. The sap from the bush comes via the pumphouse to three 5000-gallon tanks (imagine 5000 milk jugs), then is pumped into the second floor of Jean-Claude's sugarhouse and spit out into another holding tank. From there it flows down to the reverse osmosis machine, or "RO," as everyone in the business calls it, a high-tech piece of wizardry of two tanks with membranes that separate the sugar molecules from the water molecules, leaving two fluids: a sweeter sap that heads towards the evaporator, and what is essentially purified water. The water is held in another large tank, where it is used for cleaning the equipment at the end of the day.

When it is time to fire up the evaporator (when Jean-Claude has at least 150 gallons that have been separated by the RO), he throws a switch to get the oil burners going on the six-by-eighteen foot evaporator (my evaporator at home is sixteen inches by three feet, or 1/27th the size of Jean-Claude's), and starts the boil. Steam soon begins rising off the pans, and the sap bubbles and journeys from the back pan towards the front, as it becomes increasingly thicker. This part of the operation is usually run by Sylvie, his wife, who comes out from the kitchen now, drying her hands on a towel, to monitor the boil while Jean-Claude runs around checking pans, valves, and pipes.

At the front corner of the evaporator is a spigot, the simplest part of the entire operation. After testing the syrup a few times with a hydrometer (a gizmo used to test when the syrup is syrup; it is a cross between a thermometer and a cork, and it measures the density of a liquid, which is the real test of syrup, not temperature or color), Jean-Claude opens the spigot and the hot sap pours out into a round, steel barrel with a digital read-out instrument that Jean-Claude monitors carefully. When the temperature is right (somewhere between 210 and 218 degrees) he starts pumping the syrup through the final machine, a filter press made up of a series of baffles that take out any solids (called "sand" in the business), and then into 30-gallon drums. One day, his best day ever, he made 22 drums of syrup, or 660 gallons (my daughter and I, boiling all day, can sometimes make one gallon in a day).

The final problem for the northern Maine sugarer is the market. Bob Smith of Skowhegan, perhaps the only sugarer in the northern camps making his living entirely from maple, is able to do so in part because he's been at it since 1964, and because he has the golden goose, LL Bean, to whom he has sold maple products since 1978. But there are only so many LL Bean's in the world, and for the rest of the sugarers finding markets is a constant struggle. Jean-Claude recently hooked up with a distributor in Portland who will use some of his syrup for salad dressings and marinades. He has experimented with packaging maple into glass bottles with unusual shapes that have been etched with his name or the name of a customer. Another alternative is to sell the syrup in bulk to places like Maple Grove Products in Vermont, or Bascom's Sugarhouse in New Hampshire. Agents of the big buyers come around during the season and haul off the barrels of bulk syrup. There is some grumbling about the prices, but the sugarers have few options. There are no retail outlets up here, and taking the syrup back into Quebec is cumbersome because of the border. The St. Zacharie gate is a private gate and has no customs officers, so every time Jean-Claude needs to bring anything into Maine, he has to drive the 20 miles up to the St. Aurelie gate to have it inspected by Customs, then drive back down to the St. Zacharie gate.

In the afternoon Sylvie and the three youngest Paré children appear. School is out for the day in St. Zacharie and the children have crossed the border to watch the boil and see their father. The children come out when they can, and Jean-Claude goes home to St. Zacharie if the sap isn't running, yet there are still long separations, many nights spent apart. It is even worse for some of the other sugarers; Bob Smith, for instance, sometimes doesn't get home for weeks.

The Parés are charming children, pleasant and good-natured and shy in a way that seems an outgrowth of the sugarcamp itself; I am reminded of the difference between a farm family and most others. The youngest, Stephanie, runs from the boiling room into the attached apartment for cups once the evaporator is running. I'm not sure what the cups are for until she comes back, sticks one under the spigot, and cradles a cup of hot syrup, as though it were hot chocolate. We stand around sipping our cups of hot syrup, which I am surprised to realize I've never done before.

After dinner and while the children go to bed in the camp's loft, Jean-Claude and I go over the economics of sugaring. Somerset County produces the most syrup of any county in the nation, and the '99 crop had been the largest ever (the '00 season would be larger still), with 195,000 gallons made in Maine. Yet by the end of the season two of the camps will be put up for sale by sugarers who couldn't make a go of it, and Jean-Claude, who made about 7600 gallons of syrup in '99 (and roughly the same in 2000), used most of the profit to pay debts.

Even so, Jean-Claude and the other northern sugarmakers are like gold miners, hoping for that big payday just around the corner, next season, soon; when the conditions will be perfect, the market will be good, they'll still have a lease, the timber companies won't have decided to cut their trees, and the moose stay out of the bush. Then, they say, they'll have some real money, pay off their equipment, and make a living from the maple. It is Jean-Claude's dream. Does he think he will make it? He laughs. "I have no choice. It is for that I try to find the market for the maple, yes?"

The Masters of Whitewater
(1987)

Consider the Cribwork, Maine's only commercially rafted class V rapid (that's on a scale that ends in VI, or "unrunnable"). The Cribwork is located on the West Branch of the Penobscot River, and it's New England's toughest stretch of raftable white water, a maze of boulders and narrow channels. The water seems to move faster here than anywhere else on the Penobscot, and the rocks are all in the wrong places, which means that once launched, you have little time to ponder moves or correct mistakes.

To no one is this clearer than it is to Bill Dallam, river manager of a white-water outfitter called Eastern River Expeditions. Last May, on a drizzly, gray Friday, Dallam was explaining the Penobscot's personality to an audience of thirteen attentive white-water guides and one writer. Scouting the route from Vulture Rock, we were preparing to run the Cribwork.

"You want to be in the green water in that tongue," Dallam shouted over the roar of the water, and everyone looked intently in the direction he was pointing. "Then keep a ferry-left angle going into this curler here and drop through the first chute. You've got to make your move right there—to go either right or left of the Guardian Rock. You want to stay off the wall on the right, but see the way the water pillows up there on the wall? It'll force you down onto Guardian if you're not careful. Once you clear Guardian, line up for the last drop and you're done."

Some of the guides with us that day had run the Crib many times and would only be fine-tuning their moves. But about half of the group were there to learn the rapid, one small step in the surprisingly lengthy process of becoming a *bona fide* white-water guide in the State of Maine.

We had left Greenville early that morning to travel the forty-five minutes through Great Northern Paper Company land to a place called Big Eddy, just below the Cribwork. The plan was to make as many runs as possible through the Crib before the weather, water, and tension took their toll on everyone. "It would take all season for new guides to get their runs in if we didn't do it this way," Dallam told me. Dallam, who has a long blond beard and the slow, wry grin that every good outdoors guide must have, has been running rivers in various kinds of craft since he was twelve. His rafting career began in a manner typical of the way many guides find their way into the profession. "I was kayaking in West Virginia in nineteen seventy-six," he said, "and this guy floated up on a raft and offered me fifty dollars a day to paddle along and pick up people when they fell out of the rafts. Being a little short of cash at the time, I accepted." From this job Dallam eventually moved into full-time guiding, joining Eastern River Expeditions in the early eighties.

Dallam took the Maine guide test in 1981. "At first the state tried to ignore white-water guides," he recalled. "Then they decided we had to be licensed, just like the hunting and fishing guides. But they didn't have a test for us, so they used the same test as they used on the other guides. I remember one question was, 'What do you do if your sport is in the woods and cuts his leg with an ax?'" Of today's separate test for white-water guides, he said, "It's necessary, I suppose, except that we end up spending our time teaching the new guides how to pass the test, not how to be better guides."

At Big Eddy we changed into the day's work clothes: polypropylene long johns, wet suits, wool, and helmets. After Dallam pointed out the preferred run through the Cribwork ("the company-approved run," Sandy Neily, the outfitter's manager, had told me earlier), the cram course began. Leaving one of our group below to signal the second raft when the first raft had made it through, we trudged back upstream rather silently, each of us making a last-ditch attempt to memorize the river.

The veteran guides manned the first raft, a bright orange craft eighteen feet long. The inexperienced among us loaded into the second one, with Dallam as our leader and protector. From the second raft we watched as the vets paddled toward a horizon-line on the river, beyond which the water disappeared in spray. Their raft slid nicely into the chute, appeared a moment later when it rode up on top of a wave, paddles flailing in the air, then disappeared. When we got the signal from our lookout, we headed into the current, moving gently at first, then gathering momentum as the river took hold of the raft and swept us toward the lip of the first chute.

There is a distinct feeling you get when you're perched at the top of a rapid, a pleasant, helpless feeling that comes from the awareness that you're in the grip of an irresistible force. It's a kind of vertigo, and it distorts perception, causing time to stretch and bend. What may look from shore like a sluggish vessel bulling ungracefully through the waves becomes, aboard the raft, a frenzy of scattered images: roaring water, the raft itself, a tilting sky, shouts, rocks.

Only later could I collect the images: we dipped smartly through the chute, got trapped in an eddy on the far wall, bounced out of that and slid into the main drop backwards, an unaesthetic but perfectly acceptable way to take the drop, and whether the run lasted several seconds or several minutes is hard to say. Everyone on the raft, however, including Dallam, considered the run a blazing success.

For the rest of the day, each rookie guide took turns calling the commands from the back of the raft for the other paddlers. Some trainees were more in command than others. On one run the novice calling the moves got flustered and began shouting conflicting commands so fast—"Back paddle! Forward! Back left! Forward! Stop! Forward!"—that all of us were paddling independently, and somewhat frantically, as we bounced down the rocky left side of the rapid. Still, we made it intact.

We ran the Cribwork twelve times that day, pulling the rafts out of the water, loading them on top of a van, and carting them back upstream after each run. By late afternoon the guides were staring blankly at the river before getting into the rafts, eyes glassy with fatigue. It had rained off and on for hours, and there was never an opportunity to get dry or entirely warm until the end of the day.

But gradually, as we peeled off our polypropylene and soggy wet suits, our spirits lifting correspondingly, the new guides began to total up the runs they'd made and how many more they'd have to make before they'd be ready—if Bill Dallam approved their work, and if they could pass the exam—to become Crib guides.

That night I had dinner again with Pat Dorian, the Game Warden. Dorian helped develop the first guide licensing test, and he still serves as one of the six wardens who rotate duty on the Guide Board. If Dallam is what a guide should be, then Pat Dorian is what one expects of a Maine warden. A soft-spoken, sturdy man, he has a loyal black Labrador named Jake, is devoted to his work, and has seen more accidents at the Cribwork than he cares to recall, including at least one near fatality. ("A whole boatload of people got bounced out at Guardian, and this woman went into the boulder pile and disappeared. I could see her head a foot or two underwater, and I thought, 'We've got a dead one.'" Fortunately, the woman suffered only cuts and bruises.)

Naturally enough, Dorian sees the guide testing process from a different perspective than do the outfitters and guides themselves. "The testing process," he said, "forces people to know what we want them to know. Guides get molded on the basis of what we are looking for, and the outfitters have responded to that in their training." He expects that as time goes by, being a guide in Maine will be an increasingly prestigious position in the insular world of white-water rafting, in no small part because of the exclusive club that licensing creates—a club with only 373 members to date.

Already, in a state that can't boast the long rivers, famous rapids, and white-water history of the West, and which as recently as four or five years ago had to import its guides from West Virginia and elsewhere, the quality of the guides has become a source of some pride to Dorian. "I am so impressed with the guides now," he said, pushing away a plate of fried clams he had just devoured as we sat in the Leisure Life Lodge in Greenville. "So impressed. And they'll keep getting better and better. They'll be able to make moves at places like the Crib that we wouldn't have dreamed of five years ago."

Paradise Lost

(2007)

One day in February I went to get firewood. I took the canvas wood-hauler out of the wood bin and walked through the three parts of the house—main house, mud room, work room—to the barn where the wood pile is, or was.

Every spring I order firewood from my wood man, Milton. We have a routine, a ritual, Milton and I. I call and announce myself and location: "Hello, Milton, this is Michael, on the Old Jay Road." I pause for just a moment to see if there is going to be a greeting, a grunt even. He usually says, "huh," as though he's been expecting my call and at last it has come.

"It's about time to get some wood, Milton, I guess," I'll say.

We'll agree on this and other things for a while, back and forth, then agree on an amount and a delivery time. It used to be nine cords, at $80 a cord, cut, split into 16-inch lengths, and delivered. Now, because we've added an oil furnace, I buy less wood, but these days the wood costs more. No matter what day I tell him I want it, the load will appear early the next morning, before I'm out of bed, his wood truck in the road, waiting for me to move my car so he can back up to the barn and dump the cord and a half using the hydraulic lift on his truck.

Last spring he brought four and a half cords, three truck loads—the first two went inside, the third I stacked beyond the barn to air dry. It was the remains of these truck loads I was staring at from the top of the steps in late February, wood-hauler in

29

hand. Disquieted, I looked at the wood, then walked along some planks laid on the ground and put four pieces of wood into the hauler and counted the remainder. Only sixteen pieces. I looked around to see if I'd missed any. I thought about the calendar: late February. Sixteen sticks would last a few days, maybe, if the temperature didn't plunge.

I don't have to burn wood. After all, we have the furnace. But I want to burn wood. As I stood there on the floor of the barn, confronted by my miserable wood pile, I was having a visceral reaction, not a rational one. I was <u>bothered</u>, irked, troubled, irritated—that lack of wood was depressing. It dawned on me that I was right to feel that way: For thousands of years it had been my ancestor's task to do whatever necessary to stay warm, and almost always doing so by burning wood. I was nothing but a testament to millennia of shared history by northern, Teutonic peoples, specifically men. I was living out my gendered, environmental destiny, which had left in me a residue of this wood-anxiety. No wood in cold weather meant suffering, death; meant I was a failure as a man. I was aware of all of these things, the reasons why I might be disquieted, the better reasons for why I didn't have anything to worry about—twist the thermostat, heat the house. But no amount of rationalizing could rescue me from this feeling.

I could have ordered more wood right then, called Milton and asked if he had any left. Milton would have backed his truck as close as he could get through the snow on the drive—not very close—and dumped it into a snow pile, and then I'd have to fling it through the barn door. The wood would be green, and burn poorly, and it would be very heavy, both when I tossed it into the barn and when I carried it into the house. I didn't make the call.

Besides, it would be the wrong season, the wrong occasion. Milton and I do our business in the spring, when the ground is bare. He pulls up in his truck and slowly unfolds himself from it. He always wears jeans and a white t-shirt, out of which his skinny, tanned arms protrude. Milton hobbles, one leg straight, as though he has a new hip or a false leg. That's not something we talk about. Mostly we talk about wood. Where this load was cut, what type of wood it is, whether he found any spikes or metal in it. For years Milton was convinced his wood had been spiked, by "tree huggers" he said with venom. I didn't have the courage to tell him I usually side with the tree huggers.

I like hearing about where he cut the wood, what problems he had getting this load, as we lean against his old red truck, killing a few minutes after the delivery is done. It is early morning, the air is still, and already the smell of the fresh-cut pieces is strong, a sharp presence in the yard. Later, when I stack the wood, I'll complain about the labor, but secretly I like handling the wood, the sight and smell and feel of it.

Milton is sure I'll never give up burning wood for heat. After I told him I was getting the furnace, and wouldn't need as much firewood in the future, he gave me a smug smile, his false teeth dazzling in the early morning spring sun. "Ya'll never give it up," he said, nodding his head. "It's not the same—ya never forget what it's like to heat with wood."

Milton is gradually turning the wood business over to his son, and I'm sorry. I'll miss him when he stops bringing my wood. Milton and his wood are bound up in my idea of Maine. They are the Maine that in my professional life I don't see: I don't handle enough wood, and I don't encounter many native Mainers, especially ones who are connected to those things—the forests, the ocean, the ponds and mountains—that is the Maine I want to live in. People like Milton keep that Maine alive for people like me.

Killing By Pointing
(2011)

I am looking, and seeing, but I don't know what I'm seeing, so I keep on looking. I am standing on an art canvas, a religious site, a good place to while away the time. It is a cool day in November, not yet cold, that point in November when Mainers still welcome winter, still feel brave and as though the winter is a welcome challenge, before being crippled by it and begging for mercy in March.

The rock I am standing on is on the shore of Grand Lake Stream, that short, lovely waterway that is famous among fishermen in the northeast. Once one of the great fishing streams in the country, home of land-locked salmon between Grand Lake upstream and Big Lake down, the stream was also once the obvious pathway for Passamaquoddy who wanted to travel through this area before the dam was built which made Grand Lake.

The rock is covered in scratches, gouges, holes, marks. At first the marks are just weatherings, the kind of thing any rock might have, but then as I look harder—although looking "harder" in this case is self-defeating, as though the proper kind of looking is some sort of Zen exercise, where one must give in rather than strive, must surrender to the rock rather than pry too hard into its mysteries—as I look more carefully, some of the marks become regular, intentional, not the random weatherings of water and ice and other rocks. I see a line, another at an angle to the first, and another at an angle to the second, and it becomes a zig-zag, and then I see an eye or something like an eye and then I see more lines and more images and I know I am looking at something made purposely by someone.

I am looking at a petroglyph, rock art, made several hundred years ago, by someone who was kneeling at this same rock then, slowly etching away. It is an excellent spot to do such work. Even on this sunny, brisk November day one can see why this spot would make sense: there is a long view back upstream and the rock is just above a rapid, a good place to take one's canoe out to portage.

I have been directed to this spot by Mark Hedden, who should be known in Maine—if he isn't already—as Mr. Rock Art, Mr. Petroglyph; a kind of unwieldy nickname, to be sure, but appropriate, as Hedden is clearly the most knowledgeable person in the state when it comes to Maine's petroglyphs. Mark gave me directions for finding the Grand Lake Stream site, one of 13 known (or at least acknowledged—more on this later) locations in the state, yet even with directions, it is often very difficult if not impossible to find a site.

There are two kinds of people in the world: those who are fascinated by petroglyphs and pictographs (the former are images made by chiseling stone, the latter are paintings on rock, made with ground-up rock, berries, water, and other painterly materials) who will never pass up a chance to see one; and everyone else. It doesn't matter, for if you're a rock art person you don't need excuses for your obsession, which is fortunate, because it is hard to explain the fascination. I've gone out of my way to see pictographs and petroglyphs throughout South Africa, Mexico, California, Idaho, Arizona. On this day in mid-November I have come up from the south, past Bangor, then through Lincoln and Lee. I drive deeper into the open area between Bangor and Calais, past too many abandoned houses and houses wrapped in

Tyvek but no siding, and on to Passamaquoddy tribal lands, and past the sign for someone who is selling "Handmade pewter."

I drive into the town of Grand Lake Stream, which is the same as driving past a random cluster of houses, until you come to the stream, the river, and you are obviously at something of a gathering place, an economic center. There is a store—closed—right before the bridge, and an inn—closed—on the far shore, and a dam and fish ladder—open for fish—to the right, where the water exiting Grand Lake pours into and makes the stream.

The rock is on the right shore directly above . . . well, I can't say. One of the interesting tensions in the petroglyph world is between knowing about these sites, and the need to keep them protected, hidden even from the public. The public can't be trusted, is the subtext to many discussions about sites; the public will destroy, deface or even carry away rock art, if not prevented either by statute or, better, by ignorance. So I promised Mark not to tell where the site is; I had a hard enough time finding it, even with Mark's directions, even after stopping some locals out for a walk on the road that borders the stream and asking.

The man, in a hooded sweatshirt, said he'd heard of that rock, but didn't know where it was; the woman, with long black hair, and possibly indigenous, wondered if it was down by Little Falls. We fumbled around a little, trying to sort possible locations and how to get there; they were very helpful, but inexact, and I took the fact that locals have no idea where the rock is, to be a good sign. Or perhaps they were messing with me.

When I finally find it I am relieved, though also clueless, and this is just as Mark Hedden predicted.

Mark and I are at a window table of the Post Office Café in Mount Vernon, looking out over Minnehonk Lake on a grey day in early October. If there are leaf peepers visiting this day they will be sorely disappointed, as there is nothing to see but gloom.

Mark and I are having lunch and talking petroglyphs. Mark is a small man, giving the impression of great tidiness, compactness. He has a bushy grey beard, thick black eyebrows above his thick eyeglasses, and a full head of graying hair. He often wears a fleece vest and a floppy hat held on with a chin string. He is not quite reserved, but definitely quiet. He is 79 years old, a native of the suburbs of New York City, a graduate of that famous and short-lived college of artists and radicals, the Black Mountain College in North Carolina. Like many of the more interesting people I've come to know in Maine, he came to Maine in the 60s, because a friend told him he could live for two dollars a week here, found an old house at the end of a dirt road, with a spectacular view of Mt. Blue across the Sandy River valley, and settled in.

Mark is hard of hearing, possibly the result of a sinus infection in infancy. "Who knows?" he says with a slight shrug. "People used to think I was stupid, slow, because of my hearing," he tells me with a bit of a twinkle, since we both know that's not the case. I ask him how he got interested in petroglyphs. In the careful way Mark has, he tells me, "I had a high school teacher who had a lot of old books in his classroom, original texts, and he told me to go ahead and read them. I did. But I got frustrated by the fact the story stopped with European history, at the 1600s. No story from before then. Petroglyphs are a way of getting at that 'pre-history'." After college, in the mid 50s, he helped out with an archaeological study at the Missouri River Basin in South Dakota, and then in the Columbia River Gorge in the Pacific Northwest. This is when he first began seeing petroglyphs, "but it took me twenty years to figure out how to deal with them."

It was Mark who told me that looking at petroglyphs without preparation was a waste of time. In fact, he implied that it was more than a waste of time, that it might be an outrage. "I don't encourage visitation at all," he says, "at least not without considerable orientation beforehand. It's not just to protect the site, but to help people understand what they're seeing." And indeed, "seeing" is exactly the issue, as one often doesn't see what one is looking at. You realize that there is something there, but you don't know what it is, and if you do know what it is, you don't know what it means, and if you know what it's supposed to mean, you don't know what that meant to the creator of it, and even if you know that, you still don't know what those lines in rock mean in their entire context.

So does that make petroglyphs "art," an expression of the artist, open to interpretation? After all, one of the ways that petroglyphs and pictographs are referred to is as "rock art." The other school of thought is to consider them as sacred, religious images. Indeed, the dedication page in one book on New England petroglyphs refers to "artists and keepers of the sacred" which nicely captures the tension between thinking of the images, or "ideographs," as art or as religion.

Deciding which they are turns out to be complicated. Mark takes his time composing an answer; in fact, it isn't until he sends me an email months later that I understand.

" 'Art' comes with baggage in our society. In Western Europe, around 1200 AD, the sense of the invisible invincible spirit in the church murals gave way to sensual and secular realism. The psychological import of that realism is a consequence of the introduction and spread of literacy, and with it, a sense of uniqueness and vulnerability i.e. "mortalness" of the individual.

"Petroglyphs vary widely in skill and artistry, but what's implied in the ideographs refers to the 'power' an individual achieves through making himself 'worthy' of receiving 'power.' The 'power' of the self comes from the connection with others."

In other words, more sacred than artistic.

Mark adds, at a later lunch at the Post Office Café, when Lake Minnehonk is frozen, dotted by ice houses and people walking their dogs on the frozen surface, that "I hesitate to use the term 'art' because the sacred gets buried if you do."

There are only 13 known sites in Maine, or at least that's the official word; I sometimes wonder whether those in charge of petroglyph knowledge in the state have their own list, that you can see only if you know the secret handshake. In any case, 13 is the public number. One assumes there must be others, so far undiscovered. "It is safe to assume there are others," Mark agrees, "only we haven't ever found them. They may get found, probably not in my lifetime," he says, a bit mournfully. Those others that have yet to be found are not really "lost" waiting to be "found" Mark says around a spoonful of soup. "They were found once, someone knew where they were, but now they've been lost, and are waiting to be found again."

Maine has the best preserved sites in New England, Mark says, and he has developed a theory about the locations in which most of the sites are found: "They are in areas with special qualities, quite often at jumping off points for hunting, places where one might leave from to go hunting," Mark says, pushing aside his soup bowl. "They're not inside of settlements, but just outside. I think it's interesting that they aren't inside of known settlements, as though they are not part of that ordinary life." Mark pauses, reflecting. Mark's pauses can be lengthy, and one learns to wait through them.

Later, Mark describes in an email a visit to another dramatic spot, the cluster of sites on the edge of Machias Bay, near Machiasport, where the Machias River meets the Bay. He had gone there for a meeting of the committee that helps protect the site and described a ceremony:

"Just back from the gathering on Machias Bay. The tone was upbeat and positive despite the economic bad news... which, of course, is no news to the Passamaquoddy. We had a large 'talking circle,' using a long piece of driftwood for a 'Talking Stick.'

"I think I told you about my daughter, Jessie, finding it on the shore below one of the major petroglyph sites in 1996 and how we used it at the closing of the Conference then taking place at the University of Maine at Machias. At that time, the Passamaquoddy (and other Native American participants from Canada) were suspicious. Some were openly angry and aggressive. Others were very reserved. The mood changed as each speaker held the 'Talking Stick' or listened in silence. At the third circuit, the most aggressive speaker, who had originally held up the 'Talking Stick' to ridicule ('Who made this ugly thing?' while sitting right next to Jessie), called it the most beautiful thing he'd ever seen!

"We used the same stick [at this meeting in September of 2008] and only did one circuit among about twenty or twenty-five participants. The mood was entirely different but no less emotional. One young woman, who had been very aggressive at another academic conference I participated in, gave a strong performance lasting fifteen minutes. During this, swaying back and forth, she said that 'bad times' were ahead and we must pull together and work together."

It is the Machias Bay site—known as Birch Point—I am to visit in July of 2007, where the oldest petroglyphs yet found in the state are located, etched 3000 years ago. As Mark promised, there will be an orientation of sorts before we go out to the site, so the Fundy Chapter of the Audubon Society, a group of about 40 locals and summer people, gathers at the Cobscook Community

Learning Center building in Lubec on a soft summer evening to hear Mark give a talk and to view the video he made on rock art in 2004, called "Song of the Drum."

Mark begins by explaining how the Birch Point site came to be protected. It is a complicated story, "A property with a major petroglyph site (62.1) [the numbering system used by the state to record sites] was put on the market at a price of 1.5 million dollars. A local agent of the Maine Coast Heritage Trust became interested and suggested that a proposed subdivision on the property be used as a basis for safeguarding the shoreline petroglyphs by swapping 300 acres of undeveloped shore owned by the Passamaquoddy Tribe for six acres of the Point that had the petroglyphs and which controlled access to the site. Don Soctomah [Tribal Historic Preservation Officer for the Passamaquoddy] was instrumental in persuading the Tribe to go along with the deal and working with the agent and other members of the Committee to see it through. The original property owners retained the family house with five acres on the north corner."

We are told what we will see if we get up early and join the others going out to the site in the morning, then we watch the video and ask a few questions. The video tells us that the rocks on which images were carved are "a house, open to the spirit beings," and that one image captured in the video was of a shaman, or "Medo'win," whose arms were gesturing in a fashion called, "killing by pointing."

What a wonderful phrase, a wonderful concept, a great skill to have: killing by pointing, and I vow to find out what it means some day.

"Some day" turns out to be months later. Mark explains in an email that

"This is a feature of late prehistoric and historic petroglyphs at Embden and is not clearly represented at

Machias Bay. This seems to be a 'power' demonstration by Medo'wins who express their ability to bundle and shoot their 'power' into the body of another Medo'win with less 'power'. The 'victim' in public performance, would fall down 'dead' until later revived.

"The performance sounds much like the game of 'Cowboys and Indians' I can remember playing with neighbor kids (If you are a 'Cowboy' you may be wounded but continue 'shooting,' holding one shoulder or something. If an 'Indian,' you are supposed to fall dead, being the 'weaker' one.). The Medo'win performance 'of killing by pointing' was still practiced among Algonkian Ojibwa groups around the Great Lakes during the 19th Century. I have wondered whether the introduction of guns by Europeans was the inspiration?"

The next morning we meet at a parking lot on the campus of the University of Maine at Machias to share cars in order to reduce the traffic out to the site. We drive east out of town, past Machiasport to a place where we can see many directions at once. It is a lovely morning, the fog and clouds having mostly burned off, and once we park at the end of the road, we can see the town of East Machias across the way, and even across this narrow part of the bay to Holmes Point, where another petroglyph site is located. Mark gathers us together after our cars are parked and the group of us, perhaps 15, head off through a field of tall grasses to where the field ends and the rocky shore begins. Right there is a stick-built, half-dome structure. I don't think anything of it, assuming it is some child's summer shelter, but Mark stops us and explains. It turns out to be a sweat lodge, constructed as part of the ceremony that included the official transfer of land. Mark says that you don't take down the sweat lodge, you let it fall down, so this half circle of sticks will be here for some time to come. Now I notice that there are ribbons dangling from the center of the dome, and sticks hammered into the ground on either side, with ribbons tied to the tops of them, an obviously purposeful design.

We shuffle down from the bluff to the exposed rock on the seashore. Long sheets of rock extend from the bluff into the ocean, formed in humps, like beached whales. They seem unremarkable, but a small group of us has gathered on one, with Mark at the center. Mark is explaining something but I am looking, and like usual, not seeing. I look up, though, across the Bay, and see the opposite shore, and the pines on the point just to the south of us, and think what a lovely spot to do such work, and suddenly I have an image of a Sunday painter, in Boston Common or on Cape Elizabeth, setting up to examine the landscape, and to capture it, respond to it, on canvas or watercolor paper. I wonder if this is part of the impulse of these carvings, to respond to something about the landscape. After all, these carvings always seem to be in gorgeous locations, providing superb views. All of the ones I've been to in Maine are on the edges of waterways (and, indeed, all the known sites <u>are</u> on such spots, according to the most authoritative text on the subject, *Picture Rocks* by Edward J. Lenik, published in 2002), and these are inspiring spots.

Later I ask Mark about this theory of inspiring landscapes, and it turns out that I'm partially right. "Oh yes," he says. "These spots are carefully chosen . . ." But they are also "religious sites," he corrects me. "The carvings are almost certainly done by shamans, who enter into a trance, a preparation for a visionary experience. The Medo'win had to identify with the locale."

One other thing troubles me while I'm standing on the shore midway between Machiasport and Bucks Harbor: how does he know? How does Mark know what these images mean, and even which are real carvings, and which are random wearings of weather and water? I've looked at a lot of petroglyphs now, and I'm still not sure which are real and which are my imagination, and even when the "real" ones are pointed out to me, I have a hard time being sure that I'm seeing what I'm supposed to be seeing, and an even harder time knowing what the figure is, or means. If it is something representational, like a human or a large animal, then at least I can tell what the image is, even if I don't know what it <u>means</u>. But the images are rarely so obvious.

For example, I'm standing on this rock at Birch Point and I see many lines criss-crossing the rock, which is sedimentary, perhaps a type of shale. Untrained as I am, the lines seem at first unintentional, but then I realize I have to look past those weathered fractures and cracks, to the pitting beneath them, and slowly an image starts to show. From my position standing beside the rock, it is an upside-down image, of an animal, probably a deer (Mark is occupied with others, so I can't ask him). It has a distinct body, distinct legs and head, a distinct antler set, but I can't tell if it is a moose rack or a deer rack, or something else altogether. The image has been formed by pitting, what is called "dinting," repeated pounding with something with a sharp end that is harder than the rock being pounded. On another rock I can see, more clearly, straight lines capped with a little ˆ and I have to go to the other side and try to figure out which way to read this: is the ˆ on top or on the bottom? It turns out this is a figure of a Medo'win and that ˆ is its head.

How does Mark know who made them? Not only which tribe, but what type of person was responsible for them? He says it is a Medo'win who made them, and that they were used "as metaphors of the spirit quest or to help memorize the chants." But how does he know? There is even disagreement among the experts about what the images mean. I notice in *Picture Rocks* that Lenik rather chippily disagrees with Mark's claim that one image is anthropomorphic, saying "I disagree with this interpretation . . . it more likely represents an owl" (60). About another image, he says Mark "indicates this figure corresponds to a

Medo'win sign for a ceremony on initiation." Yet Lenik says the figure "represents a vulva" (58). Vulva or initiation ceremony symbol: that's quite a gap in interpretations.

One wonders what anthropologists base their interpretations upon, and whether they are just making it all up. Of course they aren't, but it begins to seem like an "in the eye of the beholder" kind of thing. I look at some lines and I don't see anthropomorphic or representational, and if I'm seeing some purely abstract image, symbolizing a ritual of initiation, for example, then I really have no clue. Mark later writes,

> "There are no single interpretations that are 'bulletproof.' It is always a best fit within what we know of how the Passamaquoddy expressed themselves within their language and stories. For example, the language we speak is part of the Indo-European language family. We have a grammar that distinguishes between active and inactive in terms of gender, male/female. How much has this affected values and social orders within any given Indo-European language? I don't know but, consciously or unconsciously, I believe it has molded certain basic values we have grown up with."

The group of us, as we spread out and wander around, discover our own figures, and we quickly began to form a self-educating class, instructing each other in what we see. I think about the decision-making process to make an image just here, on just this rock. The thought raises more questions: why this spot, in terms of its location, what you can see from it, its context? And how did they choose which rock to use as a canvas? Softer rock would have been easier to carve on, but wouldn't have lasted long—but did they know this rock was the best, or was it a lucky guess? Mark says yes, clearly they knew what they were doing in choosing this type of rock, and this type of location. It seems a highly rational choice, but I don't know for sure, and again, I wonder how we know anything about them with confidence.

But still, Mark has the best stories to tell about the images. He points to a famous carving of a sailing ship, which is shockingly representational among the other, more symbolic, ideographs.

Years ago I saw my first petroglyphs in Maine. Someone told me where to find a group—I don't remember who now, or why—and during an unlikely situation—while my wife and I were on our honeymoon—we pulled off to the side of the road along the Kennebec River somewhere between Embden and Solon. I had been told that the site was on private property, but that you could always get permission to see it. The owner's house was right across the road, and people were sitting on the porch there. I crossed the road and headed up the steep driveway. I waved at the two people sitting on the porch and shouted my question, they waved and said sure, go ahead, so my bride and I headed down the trail.

This was one of the few times where the directions to petroglyphs or pictographs were accurate and easy to follow. The rock was right where it was supposed to be, the only large rock at the trail head, and it was covered in markings. Still, it was hard to make the images out, (they were, after all, perhaps as old as 1500 years) until I committed the sin of splashing the rock with water, to bring the images out. I found out later that even this slight touching of the images was considered uncouth in the rock art world, as any unnecessary wearing action has _some_ effect, even water tossed by hand. I didn't feel too guilty, but I vowed not to do it again in the future.

But the wet rock allowed the images to show up. I saw canoes on the large shale rock, and genitals of various shapes and sizes, and other images that I could tell were intentional, carved, but which I couldn't decide were any specific thing. There are 250 distinct symbols on the rock, but I am sure I missed most of them. Then I turned around and looked upstream. The rock was at a bend in the river, where one could see far upriver, as well as down, and where one could easily land a canoe, just as, 19 years later, I would notice the same thing on Grand Lake Stream—that this spot which faces upstream allows one to carve and keep an eye out in that direction, which of course is the direction that any visitors (enemies, friends, floating moose) would come from.

I kneel on the rock alongside Grand Lake Stream and try to find the images. There it is! An arm! I know it is an arm because it is bent, and there seems to be a bow on one end, and it is attached to a stick figure person. Or at least I think this is what I am seeing.

There are modern chips and pecks placed on top of and sometimes obscuring the originals. This is a crime, of course, a defacement, but it does present yet another puzzle to the observer: why do those marks have no value? And the answer is—I don't know. Is it because they are newer, because the people who made them are familiar to us? Or is it because they have no message, no purpose, other than to memorialize Bill's love for Susan? But in a strange way the new additions are depressing, demoralizing, disrespectful, and one wishes they weren't there, at the same time you can't quite explain why you validate one set of marks and not the other. As with every other puzzle, I turn to Mark for an explanation. It turns out to be pretty simple: "The motivations behind the making of the images are completely different. One is a sacred impulse, not egoistic, meant to express something important about the spirit world, and the other is inspired by more ordinary motives, not that love is ordinary," he says with a smile.

There is an unmistakable sense of *presence* when you are seeing, or standing near, a petroglyph. For me, at least, the magic is in knowing that someone sat or kneeled here at this exact spot, a very long time ago, and not just incidentally or accidentally sat here, but sat here with an intention to make something that would last for a very long time, would outlast the artist/shaman/graffiti-ist. And not making something random either, not just doodles, if Mark and Lenik are to be believed, but something that had powerful meaning for him (I'm going to go along with the prevailing assumption and imagine the artists were all male, since shamans and Medo'win were).

I don't know that you can feel the spirit of the person while in attendance at such a site (or sight), but surely there is something affecting about these places. Not only their age, not only their hint of mystery, not only their meaning, obscure or not, but their *presence*, the weight of their being. It dawns on me that part of the allure is simply the rock itself—it hasn't moved in those three thousand years, it has barely worn, it is where it was then, and it is in the world.

One naturally compares rock art to conventional art, to sculptures and paintings, and where for those traditional forms the object itself holds the meaning, for rock art it is also the context, the location. When you're looking at a painting in a museum or a gallery, you have no connection at all to where the artist was when she or he made it—that originating location has nothing to do with your experience of looking at the object you are considering at the moment. But at a rock art location you are inevitably standing on the footprints of the artist, you are experiencing the entire physical experience that the artist had, from the rock to the air to the water flowing by on lovely Grand Lake Stream on a crisp autumn day. You participate more in the art than you do when you are standing in a crowd in the Louvre.

I sit on the rock and use a twig to softly trace the carvings.

I don't know what they mean, I don't necessarily trust anyone else's interpretation of them, and I don't suppose I'll ever be able to fully appreciate their context, but I admire them. I like it that someone took the time to carve a message on this rock, a long time ago, and it is still here. Just that.

Effort

The first time I went lobstering, it was with a man named Shirley. There's a story in that, but we're talking about lobstering now, not names.

I met Shirley at his camp on Allen's Cove, in the town of Brooklin, in early September. He was going to introduce me to lobstering, and his daughter, Jessica Osborne, was going to introduce me to him. Jess had been a student of mine at Colby College, and in one of the pieces she wrote for a nonfiction class, she described her grandfather, who was, she wrote, small, in his 80s, and still lobstering. He sounded perfect for the role of lobstering mentor.

I had been meaning to know lobstering for some time. There are several occupations in Maine which are strongly associated with the state; lobstering is one. Such associations can be outdated, trivial, and mostly fictional, but the Maine lobsterman, as one writer noted, "often appears as the last of the rugged individualists. He is his own boss and his own man . . . ." Whether the life of a Maine lobsterman is any more romantic or distinct than is a Massachusetts or a New Brunswick lobsterman, is an open question. Still, as Vermont has managed to link itself inextricably with cheese and maple syrup and Ben and Jerry's, so Maine and lobstermen seem to be tightly bound in the nation's imagination.

When Shirley came out of his camp he was as advertised: short, impish, with a big smile, and he might have been 85 or

68, I couldn't have said. Having consulted the tide tables and knowing that his skiff was now floating, not beached, he loaded me and Jess into it in early afternoon on a gorgeous September day (a redundancy, in Maine) and off we went, away from the shade of shore and into full sun in the cove. I knew E.B. White, the essayist and *New Yorker* writer, had lived around this area somewhere, and asked Shirley if he knew where. He turned and pointed to the north side of the cove a half mile away. "Right there," he said, "the one set up from the water a ways." Lobstering and E.B. White: two icons at once.

For Shirley, lobstering is a hobby, something slightly more ambitious than merely doing it for fun—where a private fisherman is limited to five traps—and less ambitious than a commercial fisherman, a status that probably begins, Shirley says, at about 200 traps.

Shirley had 20 traps out that day, and his boat reflected his in-between status. It was <u>his</u> lobstering boat, but it wasn't a lobster boat, not that classic vessel tied up at harbors all up and down the coast, with its small pilot house, big hold in the rear to carry the traps, lines and buoys, plus a small, useless front deck beyond the pilot house, beneath which is more storage, of lunches and the engine.

At first our luck wasn't too good. Only one lobster was in the first six traps we pulled, and it was too small to keep. I was pleased to see that Shirley pulled his traps by hand, grabbing the buoy marking his traps with a gaff and then pulling the rope hand over hand up to the side of the boat. This seemed like lobstering at its most traditional, as it is meant to be done, at least if you're not trying to make any money at it.

Shirley's traps, like all the traps in use in the industry these days, are vinyl-coated metal. Traps used to be made of wooden slats (and hundreds of old wooden ones are still for sale at antique shops up and down Route 1), now they are all metal. The shell is only a frame to protect the important things, which are inside. The inside of a trap is an intricate and arcane series of knitted lines, as though some macramé instructor's project has gone wild. At first glance the lines seem like an Escher drawing, where one line moves into a different dimension or becomes a different thing as you look at it. But there are essentially three dimensions to the trap, two of which are made out of nylon or cotton twine: they are called the head, the kitchen, and the parlor. The head is the pathway from the outside of the trap to the inside. Beyond the head will be the bait bag in the "kitchen," stuffed with disgusting-smelling herring, menhaden, or pogie. The area the lobster crawls into once it passes the kitchen is the parlor, where the lobster waits to be captured and removed. There is a certain macabre appropriateness to the names.

All lobstermen use logic to place their traps, or so they claim. Shirley said he puts his next to rocks in about 15 feet of water. This may partly be a function of the fact Shirley pulls his traps by hand, and who wants to haul up a heavy metal crate from 50 feet down? He uses an ordinary depth finder to scout out locations, like a bass fisherman might use on an inland pond.

As we move on our luck improved and soon we had a dozen lobsters or so. Shirley pulled, Jess removed the lobsters and banded them, using a scissoring device that spreads the colorful rubber bands—looking like "Live Strong" bracelets for lobsters—so they can be placed on the lobster claws with a twisting motion. Shirley let me take a hand at pulling up the trap, which I found not too difficult, on a calm, sunny day, in a cove, although Jess was much better at handling both the traps and the lobsters inside. I was content to be motored around and observe the rituals.

On the way back in at the end of our short day, Shirley pulled up to a cluster of buoys marking his storage tank, or "car" as it is called for reasons lost in the cluttered culture of lobstering. This is where he keeps the lobsters fresh, before gathering enough to take over to Brooklin to sell. When Shirley opened his holding tank, we discovered the disembodied claws of a lobster, and a second, apparently quite happy lobster, whose bands had either come off, broken, or for some reason were never put on. This was a disappointment, as it is hard enough to catch marketable lobsters, only to have half your catch eaten by the other half.

It was also a surprise to me, to find that lobsters are cannibals. If left alone in a trap, or in a holding tank like the one Shirley uses, lobsters will eat each other when the available food runs out, which it will pretty quickly in a lobster trap. I always thought the colorful rubber bands that are placed on a lobster's claws, and which one sees in lobster holding tanks at grocery stores in northern New England anywhere within a hundred miles of the coast, were to protect the customer from the lobster's claws. But those bands are so the lobsters won't eat each other, in full view of you, standing in line at the Hannaford's or Shaw's or Stop & Shop.

Mike Dassat is short, with grey hair trending to white, a pale complexion, a heart condition, and a pacemaker. He is a native of Dalton, Massachusetts, miles from any coastline, and yet he has been lobstering for 25 years, since he was 20 years old.

Mike and I are out in Penobscot Bay, headed towards Isleboro Island from Belfast Harbor and 25 miles northwest of Allen Cove, along with Jeff Kielan, a part-time lobsterman, former state legislator, and project biologist, a mix that seems typical of Maine. We have a peculiar combination of obligations this day: we are lobstering, we are conducting a scientific study, and we are wrapping up Mike's fishing season.

The study is our first obligation, as Jeff has been hired by the Normandeau Corp. to catch lobsters on both sides of Penobscot Bay, bracketing the mouth of the Penobscot River. Upstream on the Penobscot, a company called HoltraChem once had a factory which may or may not have leaked mercury into the waters. The plant closed in 2000, but a lawsuit was filed in 2002 accusing the company of having knowingly, or unwittingly but criminally, allowed mercury to leak from the plant and thence into the Bay.

The assumption of the study, which has been funded to last six years (a number I am aghast at—how can anyone sit around for six years to resolve a law suit? Don't they have other things to do? Couldn't a wise person resolve it in a month or two?), is that along with many other species, lobsters are a good indicator species; that is, if there is mercury in the Bay, lobsters will reveal it because of their distinctive biology.

Lobsters shed. One suspects that most of us don't know this, or much else, about the strange, not quite earthly creatures. The old joke goes that it was a brave man who first decided to eat a lobster, as what would prompt one to think one could? Looking like a hard-shelled and overgrown bug you might find under a log in your yard, lobsters don't invite pleasurable images of consumption. Not only are they bizarre in shape and general construction, but there is also the matter of the weird asymmetry of their claws, where one, the crusher claw, is larger than the other and looks a bit like a head and jaw, and the other, the pincher claw, is narrow. It is as if humans were to ordinarily have different arms, one broader and more powerful than the other, and used only for special purposes. It seems wrong somehow.

Lobsters shed, outgrow their shells, usually during the summer, and are then vulnerable until they grow a new one. During this period they are "soft-shell" lobsters and tend to hide, and it isn't until their shells firm up that they start moving again and the fishing for them improves.

It is another grand morning, out in the Bay with Mike and Jeff, and I'm beginning to think that the life of a lobsterman is pretty good; the weather is always grand, the setting is enviable, and you're on your own, just you and the sea and sky. The sky is as blue as it gets, and yet it is brisk—I have on a hooded sweatshirt with a barn coat on top of that and a knit cap and gloves, and I am standing right beside the exhaust muffler for the engine on Mike's boat, the warmest spot on the boat. I'm not really hogging the spot, as Mike needs to steer and run the winch which is on the starboard side of his boat, and Jeff has to stand in the stern to collect the lobsters when Mike empties the trap, and put them into his collection bins for the study. That leaves me to stand next to the toasty warm muffler, observing. It is Halloween, getting late in the season, and one can almost feel the "any day now" approach of winter.

We left Belfast Harbor headed east in Mike's boat the *Sarah Louise* (I'm thinking Mike's wife, or a daughter, or a favorite TV character, but it turns out to be the name given to the boat by the previous owner in honor of his daughter, and Mike kept it—a nice gesture), and then to the south a bit, while I peppered him with questions. He is obviously proud of and pleased by being a lobsterman, but he is also modest, humble even. He cackles when he laughs, which he does often. I ask him how good the lobstering is in this area, and I start to learn some of the semantics of lobstering. I ask how the "lobstering" is, and he calls it "fishing." I refer to his "traps" and he calls it his "gear." I say "lobsters" and he says "harvest" or the "catch." I ask about the numbers of lobstermen, and he calls it the "effort."

He tells me that twenty miles south of here are the best fishing grounds in the state, but that where he is in this bay is "just about the worst. That's all, twenty miles south and the fishing is fantastic," shaking his head in wonder. "Out by Vinalhaven, Monhegan to Swan's Island, Eggemoggin, that's the best fishing." Mike says it is because of the large volume of methane under this part of Penobscot Bay. I wonder why he fishes here, then, rather than there. "Kind of where I ended up," he says. "My parents were here, but I didn't plan on going fishing. It just happened. It becomes a disease," he says, somewhat cryptically.

This being the 21st century—and one can't do as Ishmael did in *Moby Dick*, wandering down to the shore for a sailor's job whenever he feels "a damp, drizzly November in my soul,"—there are waves of licenses and regulations lapping at the lobster fleet. Each lobsterman out today has a license for a specific number of traps, more than five and no more than 800. The Department of Marine Resources says that,

To obtain a Commercial Lobster License you must enter the apprentice program. You may enter the apprentice program by purchasing an Apprentice License or Student License providing you are eligible for a student license. The apprentice program consists of a minimum of two years, documenting 1,000 hours, 200 fishing days with up to three sponsors **AND** apprentice fishermen must provide documentation of successful completion of a United States Coast Guard approved Fishing Vessel Drill Conductor Training Course.

And,

Apprentices may only enter a zone IF they apprenticed in that zone. Sponsor's must have held a Class I, II or III lobster and crab fishing license for at least 5 years and have the same declared zone as the apprentice.

And,

Providing the laws remain as they are now on your initial commercial license year you are allowed to purchase 300 tags. You may only purchase 100 additional tags the following year. For example if you purchase 100 tags your initial license year, the following year you are only allowed to purchase 200 tags.

And,

> You may document up to 200 hours of your entire apprenticeship as gear time. Gear time does not include boat repairs.

. . . in case you're trying to pull a fast one and get a lobster license while changing spark plugs.

So, someone who wants to get a lobster license will first of all have to apprentice for one thousand hours (or, 25 forty-hour weeks) with at least two licensed lobstermen, no more than three. This has to be spread out over a two year period—you can't cram the thousand hours into one season. The layman is puzzled: Why 1000 hours? Why over two years? Why apprentice to more than one licensed lobsterman? These seem like giant hoops to jump through.

And once the apprentices are licensed, they have to pay for each tag, which they fix to their traps. Each tag is forty cents per year, and the license fee for someone wanting to fish commercially full-time is $435 per year. You want to set 400 traps next season? That's only $600. But add "at least $50,000," Mike says, to get set up with gear and a boat.

There are millions and millions of lobster off the coast of Maine; the supply is enormous and maybe even increasing. Arrayed against this resource are the 6313 people who had licenses in 2008, or the "effort" as Mike and Jeff call it ("effort" seems to be the term for the total number of licenses, traps and lobstermen trying to capture the resource, a result arrived at by some weird arithmetic). The maximum number of traps a license-holder can have is 800. Not all lobstermen have full licenses; some, like Mike, opt to have only enough licenses that they know they can work. Mike has a license for 400, but only fishes 320. That's the amount he can comfortably fish without adding debt or stress. The total state catch in 2007 was 63,147,767 pounds, worth $280,373,467 at an average price of $2.25 per pound. (In 2022 the catch was 97,956,667 pounds, worth $388,589,931, for $2.52 a pound). Distributed evenly among 6313 lobstermen that would be about $44,300 a piece, gross. Not bad. Except for the $50,000 for the set-up.

A few days before Mike, Jeff and I set out, a lobsterman named Chris Whitaker had drowned off of Monhegan Island. This seemed like an ominous portent for our day's trip, and I mentioned this to Mike. "I knew that guy," he says. "His Dad and me took the same water survival class a while ago." He shakes his head again. It's a dangerous life, as well as a hard one.

I ask if he knew what happened to Whitaker. Mike demonstrates with the winch. "I don't know for sure, but I bet he was fishing alone, and I'll bet what happened is that he started winching up a trap"—he pulls down on the trap line, instead of up, tilting the boat to the side—"that was rocked down and pulled himself right over. Turtled." "Rocked down" or "Hung down" is when the line from buoy to trap sinks or is washed into rocks and catches securely there.

While we're out, a call comes over the shortwave which is always turned on in the wheel house. A Coast Guard alert, saying that the *Megan Dawn* has an emergency, men in the water. Their location is out beyond Vinalhaven. Mike and Jeff keep talking, and Mike keeps steering, while half an ear is tuned to the radio. Something crackles over the radio and Jeff says, "Hear that? That means they went into the water. There's a EPIRB [Emergency Position Indicating Radio Beacon] on your boat that you have to have when you're offshore, and if the boat sinks, the switch goes off and the Coast Guard is alerted."

I am horrified, for many reasons, but in particular because Mike has just been showing me water temperature. "See right here?" Mike said, poking a dial. "49 degrees on the surface." I wonder if we're going to do something about the *Megan Dawn*. But they are too far away, and in a short time another message comes crackling over the radio, and the men have been rescued (it's not clear by whom, whether the Coast Guard, another boat, or themselves) and are safely on board a boat. Mike and Jeff, though clearly attentive to the situation unfolding over the radio, don't seem to think there is anything particularly unusual about all of this. I do.

Mike mostly fishes inshore, which means inside the line between Rockland and Deer Isle, north of North Haven Island. Some lobstermen, relatively few, fish all year round, and fish offshore. Their boats are bigger, the gear is more expensive (longer lines, sturdier winches, more replacements), and it takes a certain sort of attitude to want to do this come January and February. It is a little hard to imagine, pulling traps out of the ocean on a 10 degree day, the wind howling. Of one such fishermen who fishes outside Mike says, "Stevie's not wrapped too tight."

The actions of the lobstermen are routine, which is a good thing, because you don't want too many surprises on a lobster boat. When we approach one of Mike's buoys—and the buoys come in a dizzying array of colors, and everyone has their own arrangement of colors. Mike's are pink (pink?!); having a single color is a sign of a certain sort of status, a "gentlemen's agreement, you might say," claims Mike, that means you have been fishing for a long time and are granted the single color—he approaches it from the starboard side, and doesn't slow down much. In fact, Mike keeps the boat moving in a slow circle while he pulls the trap, and after a dozen traps this is making me mildly nauseous. His theory—Mike has many theories—is that moving the boat in a steady circle keeps the lines from tangling. As the buoy slides by he snags the rope beneath the buoy with the gaff (a long pole with a hook, as most any fisherman would know, but not me) and pulls the line on to the boat, then runs it onto the winch, which has a neat mechanical device on it which catches the rope and begins pulling it, spitting out the pulled rope on to the deck. You end up with a pile of rope on the deck, a spaghetti pile that grows larger as the trap comes up. I watch the pile warily, as I have heard tales of lobstermen being dragged overboard by the lines when they put the traps back out; in fact, some lobstermen wear a knife on their rubberized overalls in case this happens, so they can cut themselves free. I have a hard time picturing the presence of mind to do this, and in any event, Mike and Jeff don't wear such a knife, so I'm assuming we're okay in this particular area. I watch out for Mike's gaff handle, too, as he pulls it straight towards me as he grabs the buoy. I am determined to maintain my warm and secure position next to the exhaust stack.

After the trap is emptied, the bait bag is replaced. Mike is experimenting with baits lately. We're using herring today, and if I were a young man, and wanting to be a lobsterman and therefore was apprenticing as the stern man, I'd be handling a lot of this. The herring was packed into bags before we even left the dock, and it stinks to high heavens, is slimy, and neither the slime nor the smell come off you easily. After we've used up the pre-packed bags, it falls to Jeff and me—mostly Jeff—to restuff the bags with the herring, which has come from Canada, since the herring season has closed in Maine, after the quota of 45,000 metric tons had been reached, and of course it costs more as a result. Mike says the best bait is when the herring have just started to turn. He beams. "Man, don't they love it then!" The idea that the herring could get any more nasty than they are right now seems unlikely.

We're pulling traps near the shore of Isleboro, where there is a huge house and a long dock on a lonely stretch of shore. It is probably someone's idea of a cottage, though it could hold a third-world village. I comment on the house, and Mike says the owner sometimes rows out and buys a few lobster from Mike, "gives me a hundred dollar bill for them. I like that guy," he says emphatically.

When the trap appears out of the water, the ocean pouring from its open sides, Mike stops the winch and fulcrums the trap the rest of the way on to the boat by lifting the upper half of it to the rail of the boat and tipping it up. Resting it on the rail, Mike opens the top door of the trap and pulls out any lobsters, which he does with a knowing sense of where to grab, to avoid those asymmetrical claws. Sometimes there are crabs inside, and once a sea cucumber, and a scallop, which Jeff pries open and cuts out and splits, and we eat it raw—cold and sweet and salty.

The crabs are, as Mike says, "easy money in the spring"; they help the lobstermen break even in the early part of the season, before the lobsters grow large enough to be legal, or "counters" as the lobstermen say. Almost every trap we open this day has a crab or several in it, and sometimes Jeff tosses them overboard, and sometimes he puts them into a bucket for his dinner that night.

When there is a lobster or two in a trap, Jeff takes them out and is in charge of sex and size. First is gender. Females are protected, or course, and there is another routine lobstermen go through to be sure they've got it right, since the gender identity of a lobster doesn't immediately jump out at you. First they look for the "notch." The notch is a triangular divot cut into the tail of a female that has already been caught. In Maine the notch is made in the second tail fin from the right side, as you face the back, the shell side, of the creature. If you see the notch, that means she is or was an egg-bearing female and she goes back into the water without question. Even if there is no notch, you have to check. Turning the lobster over, Jeff shows me what he calls the "swimerettes" though he's not sure that's the real name. They are tiny legs, about halfway up the body, and the male versions are larger, the females somewhat more feeble-appearing. It's a pretty subtle difference, but after a few lobsters I think I can see it. You can also tell gender—at least if you've been doing it for a while—from the shape of the tail: the female's tail is broader, to protect the eggs. And of course you can always turn the lobster over and see if there are eggs lining the sides of the tail. This is important, even in a fecund lobster territory like the coast of Maine. Most of the lobsters we pull up today are about a pound and a quarter. Mike says that a female of that weight will produce 10,000 eggs, but a two pound female will produce 100,000 eggs.

Next is size. All lobstermen have a short piece of metal with three flanges on it that is crucial to the profession. It is called a "measuring gauge" although I was hoping it would have a more charismatic name, a "No-Go bar" or "Scupper Onion" or something. One flange at the top gets placed on a notch behind the lobster's eye, and if another bit of metal partway down the bar can't reach the end of the lobster's carapace, then it is too small to keep, a "cull." (under three and one-fourth inches long, according to the laws of Maine). There is a third flange at the end of the bar, and if the lobster is so big that this flange doesn't extend to the end of the carapace, then the lobster is now too big (more than five inches), and has to be returned to the welcoming ocean. I ask about the logic of this, since the bigger the lobster, the better, yes? But such large lobsters are good for the genetic pool, are survivors and hardy and probably good breeders.

As a lobsterman, there are many ways to fail. Here are a few:

You can pull up an empty trap.

You can pull up a trap with a lobster in it, and find that a) it is too small, b) too big, c) a notched female, d) unnotched but has eggs.

You can pull up a trap with more than one lobster inside and find that a lobster has eaten all or part of another, as Shirley found.

The weather can be against you, and you can't go out for days on end.

The price of herring, fuel, debt on your boat and gear, all have gone up, but the price for lobster has gone down.

You can be fishing in an area where someone dropped mercury.

And you can pull up a suspiciously empty trap, which Mike does with a string of traps on the eastern side of the Bay.

So we get into lobster crime. As with all crime, there is a context, a social milieu that helps explain the crime and the criminals. Lobster crimes are the result of the ancient clash between a resource and a work force that relies on that resource. You could call it the resource-work force clash, for the sheer sake of the rhyme.

As Mike says, once the lobster fishery was closed—and by this he means the number of lobster licenses was fixed—and other offshore fisheries had been closed or severely restricted, everyone rushed out to get a license, since it was one of the few remaining ways to make a living by fishing. That in turn put pressure on the resource, and, oddly, criminal pressure on each other.

Picture this: your typical fishermen's line is always tethered to his or her boat, whether that is a line on a fishing reel, or a net, or a string of hooks. But the lobsterman places his gear, then motors away, leaving it all behind. And not only left by itself, but with a buoy to mark where it is! The temptation to raid each other's traps is therefore strong, at least among a few. Of course this is illegal and can lead to all sorts of mayhem, as though you could replace "gangs" with lobstermen, and "gang colors" with buoys (indeed, a group of lobsterman in any particular location is known as a "lobster gang" complete with leaders known as "high-liners.").

While we were heading south after leaving Belfast Harbor another lobster boat had crossed in front of our bow. His deck was loaded with traps and the captain waved at Mike, who didn't wave back. "He's an outlaw," he said under his breath, as though the outlaw could hear. What's that mean? I asked. "He takes other guy's traps," was the reply.

Later in the day, when we're pulling up empty traps off Cape Rosier, Mike says, with a certain amount of sarcasm, "These traps are always empty—I wonder why that is?" Then he shows me a rectangular piece of plastic in the side of the trap, the "escape vent," which is a way for undersized lobsters to escape. The escape vent on this trap is filled with scratch marks, showing that a lobster which was too big to use the escape vent was inside the trap at one time, but now it isn't. Even more damning is the way the latch at the top is set. Most modern lobster traps have a bungee cord type of arrangement, anchored at two places on the top edge of the trap, with a rubber-covered piece of metal in the middle that will snag on the wire mesh on top, holding the top gate of the trap closed. Mike religiously puts his clasp in the exact same spot on his traps, yet this clasp is off to one side, not dead-center where Mike always places his.

"Looks like someone's been stealing your lobsters," I observe helpfully.

Mike shakes his head grimly. "Looks that way," he says. Mike is disgusted rather than incensed about the thefts. He figures he will move his traps, and the season is coming to a close for him anyway.

After we head north from the barren set of traps near Cape Rosier, we start catching again. And now I begin to wonder about the "fishing" part of the lobsterman's life. The biology of lobsters, the construction of traps, the bureaucratic requirements of licenses and zones, and the economics of the occupation are clear enough, but I want to know how Mike decides where to put his gear. After all, as I look around here in Penobscot Bay/Belfast Harbor, I see a million places where a trap could be set, and I see hundreds of buoys already placed, one assumes with some sense that those places were chosen, deliberately. Where do you put them, how do you choose, how do you know you're not stepping on someone else's territory?

Mike agrees that can be a problem. "There's a big code of ethics," he says. "There's the 'gap' problem, the gap between your gear and someone else's, and the gap between one zone and another. In general, you can move your gear further east than further west, without causing problems."

Mike is one of the few lobstermen who moves his traps around rather than setting them in the spring and leaving them. To serve this project he has various high-tech pieces of gear on board. One device is a video sensor that shows the contours of the bottom, and with colors illuminates the composition of that bottom (rock, or sand, or clay—each means something specific to Mike); he also has a regular car-type GPS, to plot where each of his traps is. This becomes a kind of high-tech buoy, marking his locations via "lat and long," as he and Jeff say. Part of the reason he has this device is so they can have numerical confirmations of where they've caught certain lobsters, for the purposes of the HoltraChem study. It also helps him if he's out in fog. But it is also part of his method—Mike likes to try to really "fish," like any guy with a pole on a stream, to outthink the lobster—although, since they don't have brains of the usual sort, this isn't much of a challenge. He wants to find the best places to put his traps, his gear, and he wants to know what the best time of year is to place gear here or there. In doing this, Mike has to come up with an algorithm that ties together lobster preferences, seasons, configuration of the bottom, and maybe a few other things. It takes 90 days for a lobster hatchling to get big enough for it to sink to the bottom, where it wants to be, during which time it is extremely vulnerable. Lobsters prefer to shed in warmer water, Mike says; that is, in the lower layers of the water closer to shore. He thinks lobsters like clay (Shirley thought they liked rock), at least early, when they've shed, and then they like to move as the water warms up.

"I like to put out, say, five traps in a bunch of different areas, so I'll have maybe 100 traps out in the spring. You might call it 'prospecting'—I'll see which of those sets [each group of five traps] fish well, and then I'll bring in more traps to that area. Some guys do saturation fishing, a bunch of traps in a few areas. I like to improve the percentages.

"I try to fish as efficiently as possible," he says, steering the boat across the bay to another string of traps. "In the spring I started out in deep water and during the season I move closer in to shore. I try to have a whole bunch of real good areas I can work back and forth." There is a big run of lobsters in August when their shells have gotten hard and they move out from where they have been protecting themselves, and another in October, Mike says. "In shedding season, this is the only time the females breed, so they tend to cluster together. Females are real vulnerable then. They move offshore to find the consistent water temperature. Low 50s is good for them. When they move they get into crevices, valleys, which is the easiest way for them to move. So I try to land gear in those valleys." I can only imagine how hard it is to find underwater valleys; this is yet another problem Mike has to deal with, figuring out variables like this when deciding where to place his gear.

This seems like a lot of work—it is—and it would seem to be even more difficult earlier in the season, when there are so many buoys and so many lobstermen that gear gets tangled among them. It's not hard to imagine this happening, given the many lines in the water even now.

Ultimately the bottom line of lobstering is the bottom line: can you make a living from it? Mike is careful with his answer. "You can make a good <u>living</u>," he says, emphasizing "living," "but not good <u>money</u>." I'm not clear on the difference, but he explains. "Some guys put a whole lot of money into boats and gear, and then buy the toys—they get the camp, the RV, the motorcycle, and then they get into debt, and they have to make more and more money, and work the resource harder and harder." He shakes his head. "There's no one more greedier than the lobster-man, or the fisherman. Number one, they're very competitive—myself included. When you come into the dock, and unload your catch, you want people to say, 'Wow!' But you can make a decent living with 400 traps; with 800 traps you can make a very good living, but you have to work too hard. Too much effort," and by this he means the ordinary type of "effort." "We've got 320 traps out; we make our house payment and car payment, don't owe anything on the boat or the gear. We're comfortable. I don't buy it unless I can pay for it," Mike says proudly. "This boat is all paid. I don't even buy the gasoline on credit."

Of course, like other traditional Maine occupations, the lob-sterman (and lobsterwomen; there are many, including at one time Mike's wife, Sheila) is subject to the whims of the market. One such whim is the price Mike is getting in late October. "Two dollars and forty cents a pound," Mike enunciates clearly, for em-phasis (by November that has fallen to two dollars per pound). "You can't make a living at that price. That's why I'm pulling my traps now, no point in harming the resource for a low price."

What's the problem, I wonder aloud. After all, lobsters are still fetching top dollar in grocery stores and restaurants, so why the low price? Mike explains: "Number one, the global economy sucks. And number two, the U.S. economy does, too." Simple enough, but it gets more complicated. "Most of the lobster in Maine is eventually sold in Canada," he claims, which is a sur-prise, although Mike sells to Young's lobster pound in Belfast, a retail outlet for local restaurants and lobster pounds. "And over the last four years Canadian processors are trying to take over the U.S. market. See, the problem is that Canadians have built storage facilities, Maine hasn't. And those storage facilities were financed by the Dutch. When the global economy went bad, those investments in storage went bad, so the Canadians aren't paying as much as they used to, and there's no place to store the lobster, so there's too many lobster. And that's why the price went down," he ends with finality.

Later I hear the same thing elsewhere: Canadians own the processing and storage facilities, having been financed in that construction by Iceland (not the Dutch); when Iceland's economy melted in 2008, the storage capacity went away, and Maine has nothing to replace it with. If you can't store it and process it, you have fewer places to sell to, and the price drops.

"Doesn't play well with others," Mike says, describing himself, when I ask how one becomes a lobsterman. "I was never very good at getting along with a boss. I'm not a factory worker kind of guy," he says of growing up in Dalton, even though he learned welding in high school and appeared to be headed for the major local employer in town, the General Electric plant. "Pretty much everyone went to work in the factory after high school, and I knew I wasn't going to do that," he says with an emphatic shake of the head.

Although I can sort of understand it already on this lovely day, I ask what the appeal of lobstering, or "fishing" is, for him. "Every day is different. It's gambling without gambling." He expounds on the "disease" metaphor from earlier: "It's an addiction. Some days I hate it as much as I love it. It's like scratch tickets, going out every day wondering what you're going to get." He looks out the windscreen of the *Sarah Louise* while he steers. "It's not a job, it's a way of life, not a way to make a quick buck."

It is a sparkling day, the low sun glistening off the water. We chat as we go, skipping from trap to trap, about the usual things: about skiing, about the Presidential election, about Jeff's HoltraChem project and Mike's pacemaker, about what we're doing that night for Halloween. Jeff is going to his local watering hole, Mike is going to work on a bathroom project, I'm going home.

Mike is usually out for about four to five hours when he goes. He'll do 80 traps in a day, and with 320 traps out, that means he goes out four days out of every five or six. For one reason or another we're out longer today—it will be 4 o'clock before we hit the dock, after nearly 8 hours, perhaps because we pulled about a dozen traps, which Mike piled on the back deck, then found a home for a new location he had scouted out. He'd got it all planned, checking out his GPS carefully as he instructed Jeff on when to push a trap overboard.

At our last trap of the day, we find a one-clawed lobster. "When you start to see one-claws, bullets [no claws], or reds [a reddish tint creeps into the carapace] you know the run is over," Mike says, heading back to harbor.

Mike will fish the halibut season in the spring, from April 1 to June 30. He'll also do some of the professional work he and his wife, Sheila, have taken on. Sheila is the Executive Director of one of the four lobstermen associations in the state, DELA (Downeast Lobstermen's Association), and Mike is the Secretary/Treasurer. They'll spend many days during the winter at legislative hearings and at fisheries meetings, both in and out of state. Mike will also knit his own heads and kitchens for his traps, one of the few who still does, he says. This he distinguishes from "repairing gear," which he hates to do; a subtle distinction.

About that bad heart. "It's a third degree heart block, it's called," he announces when I call in March to check up on him. "That's why I gave up long-haul trucking. My heart could stop beating any time without the pacemaker. Better to have that happen on the platform of a lobster boat instead of at the wheel of a semi on a freeway."

Lobstering seems like a grand profession when the sun is shining and the bay is filled with sailboats, when the lobsterman pulls into dock and waves at the amateurs, the tourists, when he is ". . . his own boss and his own man." There is no one to wave to today at the dock in Belfast, and we tie up and unload.

After the lobsters are put into Jeff's truck, and the *Sarah Louise* has been hosed down, I stand for a minute with Mike in the sun on shore. He's looking forward to next year, to March when he will first put out his traps. The future, to a lobsterman, is always bright—there will always be lobster to catch. Plus, it must be nice to be one of "the last of the rugged individualists."

I ask about any place in town to get a cup of coffee. Mike tells me, and as I leave I say, "so what's for dinner tonight?" expecting the lobsterman's reward, the obvious side benefit for all this labor.

"Oh, pizza, I guess," Mike says. "Something. Anything."

Farmington Park Band
(2007)

Evening is settling over downtown Farmington, the first good day after a week of rain. Meetinghouse Park, across from the brick County courthouse, is coming to life: Lawn chairs sprout from the lawn surrounding the old, octagonal gazebo, blankets are spread upon it. The audience grows to 60 or so; some stand in clusters or perch on the edge of the war memorial in the center of the park, others stay in their cars. Across the street sits the local bagpiper, a mere observer this evening; strolling through the park is one of the town eccentrics, who has predicted that Farmington will soon become the new Jerusalem; summer people carry cameras and wear bright clothes and look as though they've discovered a lost culture. Now lights burst on in the gazebo, folding metal chairs are opened with a creak, placed with a thud on the wooden floor. Up the steps, between two volunteers, come the music stands, in a big wooden box marked, "Old Crow Indian Band."

It is a Monday in early June, and time for the weekly performance of the Old Crow Indian Band (the name, chosen long ago and clearly inappropriate, involves a bottle of whiskey and a rivalry with a high school band called the Cowboys). Every Monday night from Memorial Day to Labor Day the band plays in Farmington's Meetinghouse Park, under the casual direction of Mr. Stanley Harnden, who has been leading the Old Crowers for 35 years now.

Stanley—a wiry, deeply tanned logger and orchardist, who may be the most perfect embodiment of upcountry Maine I have ever seen—asks if anyone needs a water bottle from the stock he has brought. I take one, gratefully: We will play for an hour and a half, almost non-stop, and every piece of music has lots of notes, and many of us are not used to such a load. Stanley begins each piece with the simplest of instructions: "two measures then go" or "one measure in four." No one knows what the playlist is, or what the logic of his choices are—we finish one song and then after a brief pause he calls out another, each choice appearing to be the result of inspiration. When we finish a song—sometimes ending together, sometimes not quite—horns toot from the cars around the park, mixed with applause from those on the lawn. The tooting horns were a surprise the first time I played with the Old Crows, and I wondered about the history of this tradition, but no one seemed to know.

Tonight we in the low brass are killing the rest of the band, as the three sousaphones and four trombones dominate. The elderly piccolo player with cotton earplugs in the first row of the band has no chance under our assault. There are 26 players this night, which is about average. Our ages range from mid-teens to late 80s. We are well-mixed by gender, too: about ten women, 16 men. Some of us have the official Old Crow brown vest, others are in civilian clothes. Between songs, jokes sprout ("Wheah's the Canadian Bordah?" one Old Crower asks, in reference to the title of a piece we are about to play; "In bed with mothah," he answers himself). One night a tremendous thunderstorm lets loose just as we are launching into that old marching band chestnut, "The Thunderer."

Monday nights are popular with families. Toddlers career through the park, trailed by their parents, and take turns slowly mounting the steps into the gazebo, then staring wide-eyed at all the noise. They retreat happily after one song, as though it were a Herculean challenge they'd been given, and met.

The band faces east, the setting sun dipping below the roof of the gazebo and warming our necks. As the evening fades, Stanley bends over and peers up from beneath the roof of the gazebo at the courthouse clock across the street to see how many more tunes we can sneak in. It is strangely pleasing to see him resort to this paradigm of small town life, the courthouse clock, to find the time.

I am tempted to say that Monday nights with the Old Crow Indian Band suggest a simpler time, but that would be wrong, or rather, not completely right. This is no simpler time we inhabit in the gazebo, it is the year 2007 in Franklin County. We don't play to invoke the past, we play because it is a nice thing to do on a gentle Monday evening, in the summer, in Farmington, Maine.

Fiddleheading With Colis
(2018)

The bright green, tightly curled heads of the fiddlehead—or ostrich—fern, are a cult food here in northern New England in spring, one of the few wild edibles that we harvest. Yet the picking of fiddleheads is also a business; an odd one, but still, a business.

The only fiddlehead (*Matteuccia struthiopteris*) processing plant in Maine— in the country, perhaps in the world—is in Wilton, in western Maine. The owner, Butch Wells, opens up his warehouse every spring and waits for his fiddleaders to appear. He doesn't summon them, he doesn't hire them, he barely knows who they are; they just show up in his driveway one day, at the loading dock of his small warehouse across from the town park. They might bring in ten pounds of the young fern heads, they might bring in twenty pounds. Butch pays them for their haul, and they go on their way.

In this part of Maine, you see people set up beside Route 2 in May, a pyramid of green curlicues beside them, with a scale and plastic bags, selling fiddleheads. I'd always wondered what it was like to be a fiddleheader; where one went to get them, how long it took to accumulate a pile like those I would see, how they knew what to look for and how to harvest them. Fiddleheads and fiddleheading seemed representative, a symbol of northern New England culture and economy, not to mention of its native plants. So one day late in April I stopped into the warehouse to ask Butch if the season had started yet, and if one of his crew would be willing to take me out fiddleheading.

Butch thought for a minute. "Crew? I don't have a crew. I don't call them; a lot of them, I don't even know their names. But there is one fellow that might do for you—now what is his name? It's an odd one," and Butch furrowed his brow in concentration. "I know his last name is Blood. His first name is something strange. I can just about get it," he said, shaking his head. " . . . Colis! That's it: Colis Blood."

Thus it was that I went fiddleheading one cold raw May Sunday with the exquisitely named Colis Blood. When I found his phone number and called and left a message, his "significant other," Marie, called back; Colis doesn't talk on the phone much. She told me Colis would let me accompany him on the upcoming Sunday; I asked how long he'd go out. "Oh, all day," she said. I blanched. That was a bit much for me, as I knew the forecast for the day was for misery: wind, cold, no sun. We agreed that I'd meet him at their trailer, and follow Colis out to the village of Weld, about 15 miles away.

Colis is 81, a Maine native, short, round, good-natured, with a raspy voice pitched high; he is also dedicated to his craft. When I arrived at the trailer at 8:01 a.m., he was in his truck, which was running, and he was all set to go. Such ambition for an occupation that was going to keep him out of doors all day, and which was not likely to net him more than sixty dollars or so, was admirable, if a little strange.

There are at least two types of fiddleheaders: those who do it for a bit of income, who can make a few hundred dollars—even a few thousand—during a season if they work at it hard; and those, like Colis, who do it hard, but are out there for entertainment, or because they enjoy the work environment: by themselves, in the brush, quiet—fishing, as it were, for ferns.

I can't reveal where we went, because fiddleheaders guard their best spots like gold miners or lobstermen do, but I can say that in Weld we parked by the side of a dirt road and walked into a level area near Houghton Brook, which comes out of the hills to the east of Weld and feeds Webb Lake.

As we entered the brush, Colis began my instruction in fiddleheading and fiddleheads, sometimes unprompted, sometimes in answer to my questions. My first question was the most obvious: where do fiddleheads grow?

"Alongside rivers and streams after the water recedes, and under some shade trees, but not too shady," he said, walking slowly with his head down, which is the way he always walks when he's picking, both to keep his eye out for ferns, but also to watch his step. He is, after all, 81, and he's had one heart attack, five bypasses, and three stents inserted in his arteries.

Colis' description of the best area was exactly where we were. It was a kind of floodplain, where the ground was silty and spongy, having recently been wet, and the tree cover was a mix of ash and oak, but not dense; enough cover to protect from frost, but not so thin that the sun would invade and the ferns shoot up too fast, making the season pass too quickly. As it is, it doesn't last long; by late May it would be over.

We stepped gingerly on stones to cross a dead branch of the brook, then under a leaning pine tree that was to serve as a marker on our way back. "I've picked this area already," Colis said as we made our way slowly along, headed towards the banks of the brook. Still, he kept searching the ground. "Now see here?" he said, pointing at a light-colored, feathery fern. "That's a cinnamon fern and we don't want that. They're no good. Here's what we're after," and he bent over and snapped a bright green circle off a stem. I had a hard time telling the difference between the two ferns, but I nodded as though I did.

He knelt and turned a fern head sideways, to show me a brownish-black flake that dusted this particular one. "You don't want that one," he said. "That stuff shows up early, when the fern isn't ready; if you eat that you'll need to be near a bathroom." Even with this instruction, I could barely tell a perfect fiddlehead from one that might create this unfortunate situation.

I'd wondered what tools the fiddlehead picker used, what his or her equipment might be. The main tool, it turned out, was a thumb, or, to be more precise, a long thumbnail. Colis could usually just snap the head of the fern off the stem between thumb and forefinger, breaking it where the stem gave way as one might when snapping an asparagus stalk. But sometimes they were more stubborn, in which case he used his thumbnail like a knife and sliced the head off.

After we passed through areas he had picked over, and Colis recognized a landmark he'd used to remind himself of where the boundary was, he began picking in earnest. I'd imagined that there would be a field of the right ferns, that we would cut a swath through them, harvesting hundreds in each sweep. Not so. The fiddlehead fern doesn't seem to like company, or at least the company of others of its own species. There would be a cluster of ferns here, and another over there, another two yards away. Rarely could you bend over and harvest from more than one plant at a time. This resulted in considerable bending, straightening, walking a few steps, and repeating. In other words, it was hard on one's back, and my back was not 81 years old.

The fiddlehead is a dark green color, and when it comes out of its corm (the round, thick base of the plant) there might be a dozen fronds appearing at once. They grow at varying rates, so that one stalk might have a head ripe for plucking and another has gone by already. So the fiddleheader must always be selective, judging which ones are right to pick, at least while one is in training; later, it becomes instinctive.

Of course, for Colis it already is; he knows all the tricks, all the lore. He showed me one perfectly good head he'd snapped off. "See the hole there, in the center?" he said, pointing to the tight green heart of the scroll. "We call that the doughnut hole. That means it's no good; it's gone by. If I bring them in, Butch won't like it—he'll just throw them away." (I confirmed this later with Butch Wells: "A team of six go over everything that's brought in and throw away the ones that aren't any good.") Colis also broke off the stalks of fiddleheads that had gone by, or ones that he'd picked, to both identify where he'd already been, and to help cultivate next year's crop. It was as though he was both harvesting and tending to his land, even though it wasn't his (he'd had to get permission from the owner to use it).

After an hour or so, Colis stopped, whipped a hand to his right hip like a gunfighter, and pulled out an impressive set of snippers. He held it up to show me: "You need something like this, to cut yourself out of vines so you don't trip." He reached over and snipped a vine that had gotten twisted around his leg, and which was holding him in place; I hadn't noticed. Two quick snips and he was free, and he restored the cutters to their holster.

That this was a good idea was revealed shortly after. We were making our way through the brush, over fallen, decaying limbs, around trees and through vines, when suddenly Colis sprawled face first into the soft green earth. He fell smoothly and swiftly, straight ahead; one minute up, the next second splayed out on the ground. I asked if he was okay, and he peeled himself off the ground slowly, in stages. I thought of his 81 years, his heart attack, his stents and bypasses, and worried about him being out here when I left for the day. He didn't seem too worried. "I carry nitro with me; I've never had to use it, but I always have it." He got to his feet and brushed himself off. He patted his round belly, made a joke about how it fit nicely into the hollow he'd fallen into.

"Another thing you got to keep an eye out for is frost burn," Colis went on as we resumed our hunting, looking, always looking. He dropped to his knees and dug around a group of ferns. He broke off several and handed one to me. "That glossy black part there? That's been hit with the frost. That's no good either. Doesn't taste good. Butch won't take them." This fiddleheading business began to seem burdened with an awful lot of ways to be unsuccessful in one's search: too late, too soon, too glossy, plus dysentery.

I asked Colis where his parents got his unusual name; he didn't know, other than that, being of French-Canadian heritage, they might have liked that it means "little parcel" in French. I learned that his father was born "right there," he said, pointing across Webb Lake, "at the foot of Tumbledown Mountain;" that Colis had worked for 31 years as a lab technician for the National Institute of Health in Bethesda, Maryland. He told a story about a rabbit named Alex, who he'd been tasked with injecting with "hot HIV" in order to experiment with treatments for the virus. Alex never developed full-blown AIDS; no one ever figured out why.

I remarked on how long he was going to pick that day, how long he picked every day. I asked if Marie liked to go out with him. He shook his head. "I don't know why," he said, although I had an inkling, since I was standing out there in the cold with him. Then out of nowhere he said, "I lost my 53-year old daughter last October. She got bladder cancer, and the treatments were awful. My faith tells me we'll be together again, though." And then we went back to picking.

It was as though we were two guys fishing; or, rather, as though he was teaching me how to fish, and telling tales as he did so. We talked and picked and ambled slowly along through the brush. After awhile I realized we'd collected half a bag full, and it was starting to get heavy. One of his mesh onion bags will weigh about twenty pounds when full.

I left Colis to his picking in late morning; the day was cloudy and gloomy, it barely reached a high of 54 degrees and a quarter of an inch of rain fell during the two hours we'd been there. Yet he would pick for another five hours, and for the day, he told me later, he managed to harvest twenty-five pounds; his best day of the season, a season in which he picked exactly three hundred and two pounds, according to his very orderly records.

As I retraced our steps from earlier, looking for the toppled pine tree that marked the path across the dead branch of Houghton Brook, I found myself looking for fiddleheads. Despite the fact Colis had been through here, I found a handful or more; pleased with myself, with my now keen eye, I brought them home, intending to make a small serving of them, steamed, with butter and salt. But when I took them out of the refrigerator the next day, I saw the tell-tale signs of the tight head having loosened, the beginnings of a frond breaking out from its tight spiral. Now a veteran picker, I threw them away.

Butch Wells said in early May that he'd gotten about five thousand pounds from his pickers so far. How many did he hope to get for the season? About twenty-five thousand pounds. When I talked to him a week later, in mid-month, he'd recorded twelve thousand pounds. "Halfway there," he said, cheerfully. Butch didn't seem worried about making it to the goal. "Mother Nature will tell us when to start, and she tells us when to stop, too," he opined. As it turned out, Butch processed twenty-five thousand, nine hundred and sixty-four pounds in the 2016 season. His best picker brought in forty-two hundred pounds.

Convinced that I now knew how and where to fiddlehead, I went into my backyard, where a vernal creek runs. The ground was soggy, the canopy a mix of maples, poplar and ash. Perfect terrain, I concluded. There were many ferns, but no fiddleheads that I could see; perhaps they were there but I was still too much of an amateur to recognize them. I looked again while walking the dog along a boggy area in the local conservancy land; nothing. Apparently boggy ground and an open canopy are not the only ingredients in the fiddlehead stew.

For another two weeks, I'd see Colis' truck parked beside Pine Brook, in Wilton. I'd stop and look for him, but he was so deep in his pursuit of the fern that he was invisible. He was somewhere far upstream along the banks of the brook, up high where the water once was but now had receded, and where the canopy was broken, where no one else had picked, thinking of his daughter, his faith, the rabbit Alex, and whatever else comes to mind to a professional fiddleheader.

Two

Witness

These pieces share an obsession with those from the previous section, in that they all speak to my desire to have experiences—and for the most part, experiences out of doors—and write about them. Snow camping interested me, so did sea kayaking. Country auctions don't fit the pattern, but they were something I encountered shortly after coming to Maine, and they fascinated me, too. In general, something would catch my attention and I'd want to witness it, whether it was abandoned locomotives, or ice fishing, or tourist destinations off season.

The Church in the Wildwood for example: I saw a small ad in our local twice-weekly paper about a solstice service at this tiny church; I went one year to see what it was all about. It was such an unusual experience in such an unusual building in such an unusual setting that I couldn't resist having something to say about it.

All were published in *New England Monthly*, *Yankee*, *Down East*, *Architecture Boston*, or *Route 9* between 1988 and 2016. One can still see the locomotives in the Allagash, I believe, and sea kayaking is well-established as a Maine sport. Snow-shoeing, snow camping, and ice fishing are part of the Maine landscape, still, to greater (ice fishing) or lesser (winter camping) degrees.

Sensation of Joy

(2012)

The snow was blowing sideways, the temperature was in the single digits, the sky was clamped down like a lid of slate. So I took the dog out for a walk.

The hills behind our house are owned by several of my neighbors, and whose property ends where is a mystery to me, perhaps even to them. But it is a given that my wife and I and the dog use the area when we can, as we like. It is hundreds of acres, uninterrupted, which includes a bog, an apple orchard, abandoned sap buckets, and tapping spiles long ago permanently absorbed by maples. There is a vernal pond, several rock walls, a creek, a fox den, and a nearly even split of hardwoods and soft woods.

I bundled up with my warmest gear, strapped on my snow shoes, let the dog run free, and headed out: up the slight rise behind the house, through the Christmas tree plantation that outgrew my neighbor's ability to sell them, over a rock wall and a single strand of rusted barbed wire, past the clearing at the top of the rise, then down into the trees.

The dog and I wandered, following whatever mysterious sense of destination and direction was at play that day. At the top of the hill the evergreens had been blasted by more than a foot of snow, their branches drooping with the weight of it, which fell so thickly still I was dizzy at the sight, as though I were trying to pass through a white, beaded curtain, but couldn't.

The dog grew tired of fighting his way through the chest-high drifts and began trailing behind me, letting my snowshoes break trail, and at times stepping on the tips, making me stumble. The snow melted to his fur, his face and ears. We were both white; the world was white.

We entered a particularly dense patch of woods, where it wasn't possible to easily pass between the trees. I stopped to choose a path—when I did, a branch shuddered and surrendered its burden of snow, on my head.

Shocked, I shook off the snow, tried to claw it out of my collar and shirt, then out of my gloves. I saw anew the snow whipping past my face, blinding me, felt the utter whiteness of the day, the biting cold. And to my surprise I thought, Who wouldn't love this?

I was now wet, and tired, and would be cold for a long time yet as I slogged back home through the deep snow. But the thought had come to me on the wind, it seemed—a sudden inspiration that this was a special moment, that it would be crazy not to love a moment like this.

Recently, I had taught an Elizabeth Bishop poem, "The Moose" in a college class. Now these words from it appeared, aloud, as though part of the sound track of the day:

Why, why do we feel
(we all feel) this sweet
sensation of joy?

The Lost Trains of the Allagash
(1988)

It is unlikely that anyone would stumble upon this place: this chunk of northwest Maine is too big, and this is just a dot, a tiny clearing in the center of it. You have to know where you're going in order to get here, and whether you come by foot or by canoe or even by floatplane, the way isn't easy, and there's not a single sign to direct you.

When you find the spot, you'll be on the narrow isthmus between Eagle and Chamberlain lakes, at the beginning of the Allagash Wilderness Waterway. You'll be on the side closest to Eagle Lake, and you'll know you're in the right place if you see giant pairs of boxcar wheels sprouting like steel mushrooms from the ground, or narrow-gauge rails twisted and left lying about, or if, a hundred yards from the Eagle Lake shore, you spot the skeleton of a wooden rack car, shrouded in moss, the sideboards dangling off the frame, the wheels resting so solidly on the rails that it is almost impossible to imagine there was a season when they turned.

Of course, these are only the signs of the thing, not the thing itself. What one comes here to see are the locomotives: big ones, old ones, abandoned in what surely must be the loneliest part of the north woods.

Side by side they sit, steel monsters facing northwest upon rails that vanished into the ground long ago. One is an 80.5 ton, ten-wheel beast, built in 1898 for the St. Lawrence and Adirondack Railroad. The other is smaller, with an open cab. Both were rescued from a junk dealer in Utica, New York, in 1926. Then they came here. Seeing the locomotives for the first time, a visitor has to wonder how these avatars of the age of locomotion got to this place, and why.

The impetus was that wondrously lucrative crop, lumber, which motivated virtually every other event of the era in this part of Maine. But a collection of trees is only a forest to a businessman, and does not become a fortune in lumber unless it can be delivered to a market. On the edges of the forest, it was possible to float the logs south via the Penobscot River, or, using the St. John, to the north and east. But here at the center, the options had always been to take the wood a long way north to reach the St. John, or, preferably, to find a way to move it south into Chamberlain, Umbazooksus, and Chesuncook lakes.

When Canadian timber baron Edouard "King" Lacroix acquired lumbering rights to the forests north of Eagle lake in the mid-twenties, he did what any self-respecting magnate would do: he built his own railroad, the Umbazooksus and Eagle Lake. Christened in 1927, the thirteen-mile track ran from Eagle Lake around the top of Chamberlain, across the Allagash Stream on a high steel trestle, then south along the western shore of Chamberlain, terminating at Umbazooksus. In 1930 the trains stopped; the forests had been stripped clear.

One can walk to the abandoned locomotives from one of the branches of Telos Road (a lumber company road), but it would be a hike of four to five miles over unmarked trails. Better still, one can reach the trains by canoe, traveling past forest as thick and rich as it was before Lacroix and his trains got here. Many canoeists start their journey at the southern end of Chamberlain Lake, either at Telos Landing or Chamberlain Bridge, paddle north along the lake, then portage at Lock Dam to Martin Cove on Eagle Lake. Following the western shore north past Pillsbury

Island, it isn't hard to spot the landing for the locomotives: when the water is low, you can see railroad ties and other debris, and there's a depression in the shore where a pier once stood.

The locomotives are crumbling now; there is a sign posted nearby that warns of asbestos contamination, since the steel skin that once covered the boilers has split in places and some of the toxic fibers have spilled out. The engines are still black, though the color competes with rust and other stains. Anything that could have been easily removed was taken long ago. Even as they sit here, massive and solid in a way that only steel can be, they seem to be slowly sinking into the pulpy ground.

Ice Houses

(2016)

Early in January, sometimes on the very first day, a pop-up village appears in the middle of our small town in western Maine. One day there is nothing, the next, twenty or thirty houses. They seem to come out of nowhere, like toadstools after a rain, last about two months, then one night disappear, taking the village with them. The houses in the village are small, yet like any house, have roofs and walls and windows and doors, and sometimes are carefully decorated inside. And these are the only buildings I know of that have a foundation not of wood or granite or cement, but of ice.

Ice-shacks (also known as ice-shanties) and the villages they create are an important part of life in a place like Maine, or in any of the other small towns in the Northern Tier of the U.S. Unlike other communities, these ice villages have just one activity and purpose: to make ice-fishing possible, and more pleasant than it otherwise would be. On our pond, the ice-fishing season runs from January 1st to March 31st, and on almost any day during that period, you can look across the pond and see fishermen puttering about in the village, and wonder, why? Why would someone subject themselves to those temperatures, the exposure, just to land a fish?

Ice-fishing is a refusal to give into winter. When you live in a place with as much winter as we have, one has to find a way to cope, and ice-fishing is one of those ways. The ice-houses make it possible to not only resist winter, but to enjoy it, to look forward to it and to ice-fishing season.

On a Saturday last February, when it was eight degrees out and a brutal wind swept from the northwest straight across the pond, the village expanded, became a wicked-cold Woodstock, because an ice-fishing derby was underway. The village, complete with vehicles and roads, swelled to perhaps 300 people, about 150 of which had signed up for the derby. At 300, the village was larger than some of the hamlets in our county, Franklin County.

I took a stroll through the village that day. The shacks ranged from the barest—four walls, roof, a window, barely a floor—to impressively elaborate. One shack was representative of the latter: I was walking by and was waved inside by a friendly fisherman. Inside, it was toasty warm, thanks to the wood stove blazing away in the center of the shack. A booth and table had been built into one end, a well-worn bench in the other; there were pictures in frames, shelves, electrical wiring for a generator, even curtains on the windows. One could happily survive winter in a dwelling like this.

The next day the village had lost half its population; by the first of March it was a ghost town; in another month there were no shacks and no trace that a village ever existed.

The Outer Limits
(1989)

There is something so gentle about riding in a sea kayak on the ocean, something so rhythmic, something so . . . unnerving. Every few minutes a wave washes over me, a wave of panic, as I realize how close I am to being *in* the water, not just *on* it, and Lord, I do not want to be in this water, not here, not now. On my third day of sea kayaking in Penobscot Bay, my life has boiled down to one goal: keeping the kayak upright. If I fail at this, I will have gone in an instant from a world where all is well to an upside-down version where nothing is.

Days spent in a sea kayak tend to be long; even short days in a sea kayak are long. This particular day had been very long, extending roughly from the Dawn of Man to the Millenium, or at least that is how it felt to my shoulders and upper arms.

That I am surrounded by all manner of islands should be a comfort. There are smooth, bare ones, tiny ledges, huge sheets rippling with forest; in total, nearly 3,500 islands off the coast, 1,500 owned by the state, and 38 open to public use. Alas, not one of them is in sight at the moment.

Much later, I will find my way to an island. Landing, I will be grateful, humble, stopping just short of kissing the sand. Life in a kayak can be a precarious business, and being rescued from it is no small pleasure.

The sea kayak is a strange beast. It is clean-burning, quiet, and able to pry and weave into coves and tidal flats where no outboard has ventured before. It affords entry into the tiniest places, and unscreened exposure to the grandest ones: when the craft slips into Penobscot Bay, at the threshold of the Atlantic, you feel Lilliputian, as if you've entered a different scale. This access is the kayak's glory, but as a Florida Keys fisherman once said, when a person dives into the Gulf Stream, she enters the food chain, but not at the top. Likewise, in a kayak your access to the elemental means that you're at the mercy of it. When the waves attack and the wind is brutal, you wonder where access crosses over into trespass, and if you've gone beyond that point without realizing it.

Wilderness travelers believe somewhere in their souls that they must suffer to earn their splendid isolation, and conveniently, sea kayaking has all the rewards and punishments any masochist could hope for. First the punishment: your hips barely fit through the opening of the craft, your feet can move only inches, your legs go numb from hip to toe, and a piece of hard plastic digs into the small of your back. But wait, there's more: the awful knowledge that should you turn upside-down you will be trapped underwater, hull in the air, face toward the fish. Suffering must have its redemption, though, and kayakers' rewards are the fantastic places their kayaks can take them. Kayaking pilgrims travel to Alaska, Puget Sound, and Baja California, but in the East, Mecca is the Gulf of Maine, from Casco to Cobscook bays.

I had never been anywhere near a sea kayak before this excursion, but that hadn't prevented me from making a few assumptions. I was sure the sport was a fundamentally different animal from its cousin, white-water kayaking. River kayaking means adventure, the thrill of whitewater; the sea kayaker uses her craft for travel. The difference, I supposed, was that between downhill and cross-country skiing, and I expected sea kayaking to be long on aesthetics and short on thrills.

It was with this load of ignorance that I started my journey on a late September afternoon, when Kip Brundage (a veteran kayaker) and I scattered our gear all over a gravel parking lot in Stonington, a fishing village at the tip of Deer Isle. Over the next four days we paddled thirty miles (not far by an expert's standards), crossing and recrossing our path until our route looked like a child's drawing of a star, twisted and pulled out of shape.

But first came the packing, a test of spatial reasoning I struggled through every day. The sea kayak is about as basic a vehicle as there is, so small that you don't get into it so much as you put it on, like a backpack you sit in. Most sea kayaks are about seventeen feet long, twenty-four inches wide, with small storage hatches in the front and rear decks. Into these, one must compress a Subaru-load of essentials: tent, sleeping bag and pad, food, stove, water, clothes, pots, rain pants and jacket, all manner of polypropylene underwear, wetsuit, camera, notebook. And a few not-so-essentials, which would hardly keep one afloat in case of shipwreck but do offer a sort of buoyancy: a pint of brandy, a pack of cigars, *The New York Times Sunday Magazine*.

Heading out through Stonington's tiny harbor, we glided on a nearly glassy surface, weaving through the small bare islands that flank the harbor. These islands have for generations been granite quarries, and have the scooped-out look of breakfast melons. In this part of Penobscot Bay, life has been dominated by granite and lobsters, and though the granite quarrying has eased up, lobster boats still roar off every morning.

Minutes after we launched, a gleaming white schooner streamed down on us, a coastal charter. The passengers calling down to us seemed so indolent, so pampered—with snack trays, call-brand liquors, and even plumbing—that my morale lifted steadily as we powered ourselves manfully alongside it. Finally they went west with the wind and we turned east. I quickly fell into a rhythm, pulling with one arm, pushing with the other, the paddle rising and falling; and like all rhythms it took me away to another place, where maintaining the rhythm was the only important thing. It reminded me of one other activity in particular: hiking. Inland it had been foggy, but on the bay the fog had shredded into patches, and both sea and sky seemed filled with islands.

Ambling into the lowering sun, we soon reached Steve Island, a spruce-covered speck, and circled it east to south to west. There was something gratifying about inspecting an island as a prospective home for the night. It was akin to the look you give a house you intend to buy, when you measure and take possession of it in the same glance, imagining what your life there will be like.

Our path on that trip was not entirely random. We were there to "hike" a peculiar type of trail. The idea of a sea-kayaking trail may seem absurd (where would the blazes go?), but in fact there is just such a thing in Maine: an Appalachian Trail of the sea, known as the Maine Island Trail. The Trail is a new creation, the result of some farsighted thinking by the state Bureau of Public Lands and members of Maine's small-boat community. The idea, first broached a couple of years ago, was to link some of the zillion—well, 1500—islands that the state owns along its thousands of miles of seashore.

None of these islands is larger than 13 acres. Many are no more than ledges that disappear at high tide, or are barren rocks. Others can't be used for recreation because they are puffin or bald eagle or osprey rookeries, or seal haul-outs, or because no one is sure yet what is there and how it would be damaged by visitors. When the numbers get winnowed, what is left are 38 islands that the state has made available to the public, including those that private landowners allow to be used: from 11-acre

Harbor Island, a spruce-forested, beach-rimmed refuge in Penobscot Bay, to Thrumcap Island, a small pile of hardscrabble rock just large enough to fit three trees and one tent.

The trail was the brainchild of Dave Getchell, for many years the editor of *National Fisherman*. In 1987 Getchell and a number of other veteran small boat skippers came up with what must have seemed like a devastatingly simple idea: Why not create a trail for sea kayaks and other small boats among the state-owned islands stretching from Casco Bay to Machias?

Inland the pedestrian Appalachian Trail provides access to Maine's highlands and woods. But no such access existed (except informally) to Maine's most prominent features—its coastline and its thousands of islands—before Getchell and his crew came along. The state Bureau of Public Lands jumped in, helping to select islands from among the state inventory and providing some funding to get the project off the ground. L.L.Bean also helped out.

The boating public has been equally enthusiastic. In the fall of 1988 Getchell printed 300 guidebooks—the main benefit of membership in the organization. He thought they would last him through the following summer. But by March there were 600 members, and more than 1,400 by early 1990.

One of the nice things about the trail is that it is entirely in the mind's eye: No sign of it exists. On most trails if you stray from the path you are committing a grave environmental sin, creating an indelible mark on the landscape. Here, when another direction appeals to you, you go, and the sea is never the worse for it. Another virtue is its "connect-the-dots" character, the dots being islands. Without access to islands along the way, there would be no trail, for what is the point of a long trail if there is nowhere to camp?

Inevitably there are holes in the trail, places where a traveler would have to stay on the mainland for a night or even several nights in a row. Of course, this is true only if that traveler is tackling a large chunk of the trail at once—a not insignificant attempt considering that the entire trail runs for about 375 miles, from rough-weather headlands and open water to tiny channels deep inside harbors and bays.

The first night of an outdoor excursion is always a cocktail of exhilaration and uneasiness, when you realize that the scenery is swell but no hot shower awaits you in the morning. I had been told there wouldn't be mosquitoes this time of year, but this proved to be optimistic. While I picked at a formless freeze-dried dinner, they mingled happily with the sand fleas that leapt into the food, my brandy, everything. But a slight wind slapped waves against the rocks, creating a lonesome boom, the right sound for life on an island.

Come morning, a school of lobster boats bellowed by, but that was the sole trace of civilization, and soon all evidence of it was gone. I decided to play Robinson Crusoe and take inventory. Steve Island is barely a good football toss long, with two pocket beaches that almost vanish at high tide. It is island *qua* island: a few trees for protection from the wind, a hint of sustenance—rose hips on a rugosa rose, and one lonesome raspberry bush. The chunks of pink and white granite that compose the island are flecked with quartz, and the whole affair sparkled in that painter's light you get only by the sea. There was something muscular about those boulders; they looked like the shoulders and backsides of a gang of cross-training sumo wrestlers locked arm in arm in a rugby scrum, a spectacle that one rarely encounters.

The wind had freshened, and we delayed re-boarding our kayaks. The water that had been mirror-like yesterday was now chop. The background music I imagined I heard was dark and low, rumbling in a minor key. But I couldn't very well suggest to Kip that we stay until the wind died—in a couple of weeks, say—so I sat down in an inch of cold water in the kayak and headed west with him.

You have a loon's perspective on the sea from a kayak, your head only two feet from the surface. Throw two-foot waves into the picture, and at times it seems as though you are tunneling through the water like a surfer through a curl. To keep the ocean out and bind themselves in, kayakers wear a spray skirt—a sort of Euro-punk neoprene garment—around their waists, fitting it to the collar of the boat for a more-or-less-watertight seal. Kayaker is then wedded to kayak, forced to share its perils. In the event of an upset, the kayaker usually bails out, pulling the spray skirt off the collar. Then the kayaker and his partner right the craft, grimly cheerful. I worked hard to avoid this dismal event, learned to ride the waves, kept my hips loose.

That morning we zigged west to a cormorant-covered rock, then zagged southeast to the largest of the state's public islands, and perhaps the loveliest, Harbor Island. From where we disembarked, the landmarks on the mainland—Cadillac Mountain to the northeast, Megunticook to the northwest—looked like huge frozen waves. Here black-backed gulls were joined by a family of yellow-shafted flickers, a jay-sized bird that flies with a flap and glide, flap and glide, like a frog kicking through the air. As I walked they swooped tree to tree, trapezists without ropes or net. The day was a late September gift from the weather gods, and we lingered in the sun.

We left this paradise the next day, but only temporarily. Our original plan had been to paddle down Isle au Haut to the Acadia National Park campground at Duck Harbor. But as the day wore on, the wind sharpened, and skirting the rocky shore began to sound like a bad idea. Gusts roared into our faces, the sea was froth, and our next move was obvious: retreat.

Back on Harbor Island, we had an exceptional evening. It was that time of day that seems so rich because it is really three times at once: night in the east, dusk directly overhead, and sunset on the horizon. We built a fire with the help of some dried kelp and brush below the high-water mark on the beach, adding some handy driftwood to the blaze. The kelp crackled, the sound of salt burning, and put off a rich, ocean smell. Like any ordinary backpackers would, we polished off a high-carbohydrate meal of stuffed tortellini shells, bagels, and chocolate bars, and then sat scrunched in the sand, as close to the fire as we could get without igniting ourselves, and watched the moonlight lift and drop on the waters. The moon laid a path to us, Mars burned low on the horizon, and the sky was spattered with stars. The moon moved slowly west, and we told stories of other campfires.

My back to the wind was cold, my face hot from the flames, but this seemed appropriate: it was the evening of the autumnal equinox, and I was still living in summer while fall snuck up behind. I began to think of the possibilities of this in-between-ness. This led to thoughts of the existential strangeness of the diurnal progression, which led to thoughts about how odd it is that the earth tilts on its axis, which led me to wonder if I'd left my headlights on back in Stonington. And then I was asleep.

Day three began pleasantly enough. The sunrise spread out like the first strokes of a paintbrush on wood. I scanned the island for the small details a small place invites you to seek: followed field-mouse trails that tunneled into the grass, then dove underground; found the carefully rendered remains of a crab. Butterflies fluttered about, and purples, whites, yellows, and greens grew among the boulders—New York aster, primrose, gooseberry, butter and eggs.

Back in the water, a band of harbor seals joined us, their round, rubbery heads popping above the surface like wet rubber balls. Harbor seals are a common sight in these waters and a welcome one, visitors from that foreign environment beneath you. In a sea kayak you are on nearly the same level as the seal, and once again you gain an intimacy that any other traveler lacks. They stayed slightly astern for a while as we paddled along, bobbing and sinking, always facing us. From a different perspective, their expressions might have looked like ones of curiosity; up close, though, they appeared to be outraged at our trespass.

Those of us who live pale, un-dangerous lives sometimes crave exposure, long to put ourselves into difficult circumstances and feel the elements work on us. So it was that in the morning I managed to wriggle my kayak onto a lonely rock ledge perched on the border of Isle au Haut Bay. There was no other land directly to the south, and the wind howled at me; I was exposed there, as exposed as I could get. I have had this sensation before—on a sandbar in the Brooks Range in Alaska, in a snowstorm on a frozen lake, on a blazing sand wash in the Grand Canyon—but it seemed the very essence of sea kayaking. Life can't get much more basic: rock, sea, kayak, kayaker.

That moment by itself could have justified the trip; but then it slipped away, and clouds closed in overhead as we set out to cross Merchant Row, a mile-wide channel where exposure can quickly get ugly. The waves were the biggest we had seen, a double-sided assault from behind and from our left. We dipped and rolled, now sinking into a trough, now rising. It was then that the feelings of imminent doom began to sweep over me. Having felt the thrill of standing open to the elements, I now craved the comfort of shelter from them. The bigger the waves became, the greater this need, until I imagined myself as Dorothy, clicking my ruby slippers and muttering, "There's no place like home . . ."

I survived, as it turned out, and the rest of the morning vanished into a cold, gray, wet haze. After the crossing, we met a couple in a double kayak, headed toward Isle au Haut. We told them what the water had been like, me in tones of horror and warning, Kip rather casually. While the man studied a map, the woman stared south like an acrophobe being forced to board a roller-coaster.

Later it occurred to me that as I paddled the trail I was sometimes blank, mindless, not thinking of anything at all. To the degree that the Maine Island Trail is like any other trail, it may be most similar in this way: that you reach that rhythmic condition in which you are lost to yourself and exist only as a part of what surrounds you. You become an object on the sea, moving with or against the tide, in among islands and trees and birds and seals, one paddle stroke after another, after the next, after the next.

For my final night—my first night alone, since Kip had to return to shore—we landed on an island with a rocky meadow, whose name I never learned but whose open slopes reminded me of pirates and treasure. Kip left and I began to harrumph and mutter, grunting the little self-conscious noises of the newly alone. A bird called a piercing cry of four notes at precisely the same pitch and tempo as the first four notes of Chopin's funeral march. Then a west wind swept the clouds away, and the sun set in an aisle formed by seven neatly arranged islands—a miraculous coda to another day.

That night I owned an island off the Maine coast. I know I owned it; no one else was there. I sat on my beach of sand and shells and watched the tide pulse in, the moon on the water, the firelight dance on the polished surface of the kayak. Off in the distance I saw another island with a tiny house on it. I don't know what they paid for their island, but I didn't pay a dime for mine, and mine had driftwood for a fire, along with ospreys, two nests, and two large osprey eggs, almost three and a half inches long, in a patch of dry grass on the ground.

While we had paddled across Merchant Row earlier in the day, the words *island* and *sea* had repeated themselves in my mind, alternating with each stroke—island, sea, island, sea— until the words settled into an epigram: *islands are the answer to a question posed by the sea.* The phrase meant nothing until that last night. Then it occurred to me: the question the sea always poses to travelers is, *Where can you find the shelter you need?* And the answer given by islands—given especially to those in sea kayaks—is, *Here.*

A Stroll in Winter
(1991)

One of the great truths of winter camping is that there is not a lot to do once the sun goes down. This should come as no surprise to anyone accustomed to the outdoors. But it came as a slight shock to me at the beginning of a camping trip to the Allagash Wilderness Waterway that I took with a friend, Tom Stewart, one February. On our first day out, it was pitch black by 6:00, and although I was far from sleepy, there was no place to go but inside my sleeping bag, where I tried not to dwell on the fact that it was only five degrees above zero inside the tent, and that we were sixty miles from the nearest town. I lay still and listened to the faint hooting of a great horned owl. This was followed, as if on cue, by the yip-yowling of coyotes upriver, no more than a quarter-mile away.

Welcome to the Allagash in winter! Six months earlier, this wilderness waterway—a hundred-mile string of interconnected lakes, ponds, streams, and river—floated more than 10,000 canoeists northward through the Maine wilderness. In winter, one finds human activity on the waterway's southern reaches, where snowmobilers gather for ice-fishing or the thrill of riding at full-throttle across the frozen open spaces of Chamberlain and Eagle lakes. But in the northern portion there is less access and, given the strength of the river current, much of the ice is too fragile to support the weight of the machines. Thus snowmobilers, or visitors of any sort, rarely venture here.

Winter is an exhilarating time for camping because winter isolates every element of experience. Any movement seems dramatic, because so little moves; every sign is important, because there are so few signs; each sound is an event. On our second morning out we towed our toboggan and gear north to Round Pond, a two-square-mile bulge in the northern portion of the waterway some thirty-five miles south of its confluence with the St. John River. Our original plan was to travel across the pond and down the Allagash as far as we could go, but this itinerary was thwarted by a day of unseasonably warm temperatures that transformed the ice at the outlet to Round Pond into open, swift-running water.

While Tom and I debated what to do, we looked back and saw a white-tailed deer detach itself from the evergreens and begin moving tentatively across the pond. Behind this solitary scout, groups of two or three or six deer stepped diffidently onto the ice, walking gingerly. They then got wind of us and all stopped in midstride. We studied them; they studied us—foreigners in their frozen world. Then they bounded off across the lake in that odd, stiff-legged deer trot, which seems at once to be flight and an attempt to maintain composure.

After the deer, we decided to forego the dubious pleasure of trying to drag our gear downstream and elected, instead, to make a base camp on this pond. Why not? This seemed as good a wilderness theater as any from which to observe the drama of nature.

We were not disappointed. After setting up our tent, we went exploring downriver on snowshoes and soon came upon an otter playing on an island in mid-stream. The sleek, dark animal took center stage as we watched from our seats on the river bank. It would slide down a hill into an open portion of the frigid river, scamper up, and slide again. After a while it disappeared beneath the ice on the river and reappeared with a small fish in its jaws, which it brought to shore not far from us and ate. Later, we discovered two more otters living a quarter-mile further downstream on another island. They, too, rolled and frolicked, dove beneath the ice, nuzzled each other, and generally gave the impression of being the most contented creatures imaginable.

Coming back to camp we passed a tributary creek, which was flowing under ice, appearing every so often through breaks in the ice. Trips into the woods are like visits to art museums for me: in both cases I hope to have at least one insight per visit, to understand or realize I am seeing one new thing about art or the woods, and this creek gave it to me. The water, as it flowed out of the ice and over it, kept pulsing and changing shape, almost as though it wasn't water, but a sentient organism that was metamorphosing into pleasing designs as it flowed. I hadn't ever seen water in this particular way before, and so my trip was complete, even before it ended: I had seen something new.

Tom and I gladly returned to witness the playing otters a number of times during our stay. But we were as much observed as observing. A different day, returning from a hike, we noticed a hole in the ice and a new set of tracks. Here an otter had surfaced through the ice, slid along the snow to where our well-worn footpath led from the tent to the river, investigated our scent, and then returned to the hole in the ice. Nature, it seems, abhors a mystery.

One day I observed a strange series of tracks, obviously made by two different animals, overlapping each other. As I walked down to the lower island where the two otters lived, I found similar tracks telling a tale. A coyote had left the woods on the eastern shore and had crossed the trail Tom and I had made in the last few days tramping up and down the river. The coyote had ventured out onto the thin ice on the edge of the river, poked around, and then headed downstream, crossed over to the island, and proceeded directly to the hole where we had last seen the otter pair. Where there had been a neat hole, there was now a furious gouge in the snow, with snow heaped all around. I saw no blood, but the coyote tracks left the hole and went further downstream, crossed the ice once more, and disappeared into the woods.

Had the coyote grabbed one of the otters? Or had he just been poking about the hole? I'll never know, but what was clear is that coyotes, as relative newcomers to the northern Maine woods, are firmly establishing their roles as actors in nature's drama. In fact, they are trying their best to steal the show.

On our last afternoon, after we had returned to camp and I was sitting in the doorway of the tent wrapped in my sleeping bag and staring absently towards the river, a coyote trotted out onto the lake ice from the western shore. He appeared suddenly, and with total nonchalance. He paused when he crossed our trail, looked up at us, then moved on with what appeared to me to be self-assurance bordering on arrogance. Moments later another coyote crossed at midpond. Something was stirring. Suddenly deer scattered across the open space in speedy bursts, and dispersed into the woods. We watched, listened, half expecting a chase—the climax and denouement of the play, perhaps. But nothing occurred, at least not this day on our portion of the stage.

As dramatic as the days can be, it is at night when the character of winter camping becomes clearest, for it is at night when winter most deeply stirs human emotions with its enveloping cold and superior blackness, its profound silence. All of which leads to an overwhelming sense of isolation. The wind whistles more sharply at night and staying warm is an even greater challenge. The night sky, with winter's constellations, is dazzling or, if cloudy, impenetrable, and one either contemplates the vastness of the universe or turns one's thoughts inward. It is this combination of cold and darkness that convinces a sojourner just how far outside the human community he has wandered.

One may be able to pretend momentarily that the road isn't far away, or imagine that there must be someone in a cabin nearby, but what the camper finds himself believing is that there is no one else, anywhere. No campfires in the distance, no sounds of motors, no voices but your own.

Nights are also a challenge. After all, you have more than twelve hours of night, and the options of what to do are pretty limited. My winter camping evenings unfold like this: standing around the stove while it heats water for yet more hot drinks; a lot of talk about all sorts of things, running the gamut from the trivial to the mundane, but occasionally rising above, as when we talk about family, past tales of glory, the stars. Then reading with a headlamp: on this trip I took along *The Road of a Naturalist*, by one of my favorite natural history writers, Donald Culross Peattie. Then made notes in my notebook, including this one: "Tom and I see the same shooting stars; amazing."

The last night, after Tom and I had dissected the nation's problems (reduced, basically, to television), Tom turned in. I stayed out, warm enough at two above zero in all of my warmest gear, and I watched the cold world in which I found myself. I could turn a slow circle and admire the entire vault of stars, since not one was obscured by a cloud. I stood there so long beneath the points of light throbbing through the dry atmosphere that I could see the sky turn; so long that Mars, which had been glowing brightly above the northern horizon, dipped below a mountain. Snow camping forces one to go slow, to pay attention to things, to watch for signs. This might apply to weather, or equipment, or the snow itself. So when Mars dropped out of sight, I took that as a sign that I, too, should retire.

All in, All Done

(2010)

At first, you have a hard time telling what kind of place this is. There are cars, obviously abandoned, all over the yard, so you think used-car lot; there is an old gas pump, claiming to sell gasoline at prices a dollar and a half out of date, so you think gas station; and then you approach the building which is covered in old metal advertising signs—old Coca-Cola signs, old Texaco signs, old Muffler shop signs, old Cooper tires and Champion spark-plug signs, an old stop-light signal, Bud light and Pepsi-Cola signs—and you think auto repair, or maybe antiques store, and then you head inside and think, Pluto.

Hurrying to get inside before the 6 p.m. start at Harold's Auctions in Rome, Maine, I push open the door just as someone on the other side pulls it inward, and I am met by a fantastic sight: a man with a deeply weathered face and a wild pile of hair and beard, thick glasses, perhaps 60 years old, who pulls me inside. Behind him are two or three other similarly dramatic faces, and behind them is a carnival of lights and objects, like entering a fun house.

Harold's Auction house is a shack beside Route 225 in Rome (only one road leads to Rome, and it passes right through it, "it" being a closed general store, Harold's used car/auto repair/auction house emporium, and a handful of houses). Harold's is also a mechanic's garage. Not "once was" a garage, but is, every day except Saturday nights in the summer and fall, when it transforms from Harold's Body Shop to Harold's Auctions.

Unless it's a sunny summer evening—in which case the rear garage door is open for air and light—you enter Harold's through a narrow doorway stacked high on both sides with things. There is no better word for them than the vague "things," for there is no other word that would embrace the variety, the diversity of objects, no other word that would capture all that is there. Adding to the confusion is that you don't know which of it is for sale, and which has been sitting there for decades. On your left is Harold's stage and the office; you've entered into the middle of the auction offerings, several tables packed with those "things," the tables themselves surrounded by items resting on the floor, and more tables against the outer walls of the garage, also covered with auction offerings. Harold is a serious hurricane lamp collector, and these hang from all over the ceiling, as do even more advertising signs, although these—unlike the ones outside—are electric, neon. Most are beer signs: Bud and Coors and Miller and Schlitz. None of the hurricane lamps are for sale; Harold won't part with even one.

"What the hell's the matter with you people?" barks Harold up on stage as the auction gets going, waving his arm loosely in the air. "That's a perfectly good piece of junk," he says, sternly, and the audience laughs. Soon another item is lifted from the pile of articles heaped on tables in the center of the room, and Harold says, "Now folks, pay attention . . ."

Harold Hawes is sitting on a stool, behind a counter filled with junk, on a small stage that takes up half of one end of his car garage, where during the week he fixes other people's cars. The other half of that end of the garage holds a small office, with a window between the stage and the office, through which papers are passed. A man sits at an old desk near Harold, recording the sales, and passing the papers through the window, to where two women, one elderly, one middle-aged, tally up the sales by hand.

Harold always wears a ball cap, usually one with a "Carquest" logo or some other automotive slogan. Harold is slight, with thick glasses, a grey beard, and with the hat, the glasses, the beard, and the upturned collar on his mechanic's jacket, one can't see much of his face. Especially when the auction begins and he holds the microphone that sends his voice through a scratchy one-speaker sound system up tight to his mouth, as though he is a singer crooning to his audience. He sits with one leg crossed over the other on the stool and uses his right hand as a prop, another type of voice urging the bidding on. He opens the hand palm out, offering the item to us, wiggles his fingers as he talks, slowly flaps the hand back and forth as he goes from one bidder to the next and back.

On your right, taking up the rest of the garage, is the audience, in a dozen row of folding chairs, wedged between one wall and a rectangle jutting out from the opposite wall, where snacks are for sale. All auctions, without fail, have a place to buy food. Most are like this one, a small cubicle cut out of the interior, with a waste-high counter, behind which the auctioneer's wife or daughter glides around, making burgers, selling Moxie, plucking hot dogs from the hot dog cooker. At Harold's, the signature item is pies, good-looking lemon meringue pies, home-baked.

The audience has squeezed among each other to find their seats. When Harold's is full there may be 50 people; when it is not, the crew of office people, runners, and hangers-on at the front of the hall matches the number of people in the seats. In October, at the next-to-last auction of the season, I count 25 people in the audience, the ones whose task it is to buy the things being hoisted by Harold's helpers.

Chief among these helpers is Brick, an imposing fellow with a booming voice. Brick is large, by which I mean fat, and he wears a stretchy green t-shirt that stretches generously over his stomach, which conceals most of the top few inches of his pants. Brick is one of the more effective helpers, as he shouts out the lot number (all auctions have lot numbers, which represent where the items came from in the case—almost universally the case—when the items have come from many places, many persons), describes the item in somewhat flowery terms, then holds up, for example, the tattered old picnic basket for everyone to see. Sometimes Brick will do things like put on a blond wig that is about to be sold, for our amusement, while another runner, an older woman, tries to outdo him by screeching a description of the toaster she wants to sell. Soon she and Brick are swapping insults, and in the back of the audience I see an uncomfortable-looking couple. They are wearing clean shorts with socks and shoes, their hair is neatly arranged, and clearly they have fallen into a strange world.

Every auctioneer has his (I've not yet seen a female auctioneer in action; Pam Brooks of Houston-Brooks auctions in Burnham is one of the few female licensed auctioneers in the state) own shtick, his refrains, his verbal tics. One of Harold's is the use of "now folks, pay attention," at the beginning of each bidding round, even though the particular item is no more special than the one preceding it, or the ones to follow. When he gets rolling, when he has gotten his first bid, or even before he's gotten any, he starts speaking to us as "boys," as in "Boys, that's a beauty, now who'll give me five dollars, five, five dollars, four, four dollars" and so on. We're boys, despite the fact at least half of us are women, more than half, and most of the bids come from the women in the "crowd." Once Harold stops speaking generally, and focuses on the female bidder, it becomes "dear." "That's your bid, dear," he'll say to a confused woman who is bidding against herself.

On the scale of Maine auctions, Harold's is decidedly on the low end. Not that Harold's is unworthy, but only that if one were to judge an auction on the value of its offerings, Harold's would be sentenced harshly. But that's not the only way to judge an auction, especially in Maine, where auctions have many roles.

There are livestock auctions, and, lately, foreclosed house auctions, and auction-based securities (at least until the market for these things, whatever they were, collapsed during the financial breakdown of 2008), and tool auctions and fund-raising auctions, but the Maine country auction is a thing apart. It is a form of entertainment, a Saturday night out where the cost can be nothing, or maybe a few bucks, and the show is always new. It is also a type of economic system, where wealth—or a few bucks—and products are redistributed; a business, too, both for the auctioneer and for some in the audience, who are there to stock their shops and stores with antiques, art, junk. The auction is a resource, for those who need to clean out old houses, or hunger for some cash, and an eco-system as well, buyer and seller and auctioneer each serving and feeding on one another. At many country auctions in Maine one has the feeling that the merchandise has simply left the home of one of the people at the auction for the home of someone else at the auction through this ritualized alchemy. And auctions are an exercise in community. Many of the people at country auctions know each other, and attending an auction where you know the auctioneer, the audience members, the helpers, is like attending the local school's Christmas pageant, or a bean supper.

One could live in Maine a long time and never go to an auction or be aware that there are auction houses dotted throughout the state. But once you start to notice, it can become addicting, the lure of auctions and the thought that this time, this time, there will be something for sale that you really need/want/can profit from/can sell/will give away/ought to buy for Christmas.

Auctions have their own music, their own poetry. An auction house like Harold's doesn't advertise, except for a neon yard sign out front which simply announces "Harold's Auction/ Saturday, 6/13, 6 p.m." Most others do. The next level up in the hierarchy of Maine auction houses, Clyde's Auction House in New Sharon, posts a listing of items in the local, twice-weekly newspaper, *The Franklin Journal* ("Serving you since 1840") in the Friday edition before the Saturday sale, always accompanied by the disclaimers that "Description subject to error," and "A very partial listing includes . . ."

It can be difficult to focus on all the terms in the published list of items to be sold, as they flow on and on, a river of descriptive text, some of whose terms are a mystery, like images in an obscure poem.

> Wainscott store counter, inlaid server (missing marble), walnut work table, candle stands, 2 dr., 2 drw. cupboard, vintage server and china closet, enamel top deco table, press back arm chair, Eames chair, high back settee, ash stand, sq. oak stands, wash stand, walnut hall tree w/ umbrella rack, oak commode, set 4 caned pine chairs, Danish Modern coffee table, 5 drw. oak chest w/splash, set 4 t back mah. dining chairs, stenciled Boston rocker, pr. rose back side chairs, Empire sofa, Sheraton style loveseat, cannon ball rope bed, rampdown wood stove, iron bowl and pitcher stand w/mirror, single brass bed, iron garden chair, 2 iron garden urns, marble sink w/faucets, round tap table, very nice 3 drw. marble top walnut chest w/ ditty drawers and mirror, oak high back buffet, medicine cabinet, 3 drw. stenciled pine chest, Crosley table top radio, round oak stand w/arts and crafts look, pressed mah. stand, lift top commode, child's roll top Paris desk w/chair, mah. bow front buffet, 1 drw. stand, oak Singer treadle sewing machine, 3/3 mah. chest, 5 drw. graduated mah. chest, mah. 2 door bookcase w/column front, mah. Queen Anne style vanity, mah. lowboy cedar chest, mah. dining table w/4 chairs, iron & tile bench . . .

One can probably come up with an image of a "cannon ball rope bed" if one thinks slowly and carefully, even if one has never seen such a thing.

At the other end of the scale from Harold's, at least in terms of value of objects, is the Thomaston Place Auction House on Route 1 in Thomaston, close to the St. George river. This auction is held only occasionally, unlike most of the others in the state which tend to be on the same day (Saturday night, Thursday mid-day, Sunday morning are all spoken for). But the Thomaston auctions are huge auctions, taking at least two days, and one is fixed certain on the calendar: the Labor Day weekend antiques and art sale.

As I drive to the coast on a glorious late summer/early fall day, the Saturday before Labor Day, when the roads are filled with cars, with the last of the summer people clinging to the final weekend, and the natives reclaiming the state, I pull up at a stoplight behind two motorcyclists, a man and a woman, dressed in matching leather chaps and motorcycle jackets. As I sit at the light in that vague mental condition that stoplights invite, I realize the license plate for the motorcyle on the left reads "HARDWRK" and the one on the right reads "PAYSOFF." I wonder whether the slogan is true, and if they always ride this way, with him on the left, her on the right.

The building housing the auction is a long wood-shingled affair, two stories tall, with weird, six-sided windows along the first floor. It was once a chicken barn, then a weaving factory, then storage, now a high-end auction house. The main entrance is through double doors on the left of the building from the parking lot, under a portico of sorts. Inside this half of the building the items for bid are available for examination, before the sale begins.

When I enter the Thomaston Place building that morning, I am greeted by a man in a crisp white shirt and black pants. This reminds me that I am no longer in Rome, or at any other auction I've been to in Maine. A catalogue of the items for sale is available, for $20, in full color, with detailed descriptions of the items and high and low estimates, which turn out to be surprisingly accurate, at least in terms of the low estimate being a true low.

People who are serious about bidding are careful to come early enough to examine the items. All auction houses, except Harold's, advertise a particular time for examination, or "previewing," and sometimes the preview is the few hours before the auction starts, sometimes it is the entire day before. Previewing is an exercise in the art of looking, and it takes some practice. It is surprisingly difficult to look at all of the objects in a room with any care, to spot one you might want, and to look at it closely and thoughtfully. No matter how hard I try, how much I challenge myself to pay attention, I often will see something come up for bid that I might want, but have no memory of having seen in the pile during my inspection. And I will look at something and think I might like it, then look at it later—either after buying it or not— and discover it looks entirely different, usually much worse.

The aisles here in the old chicken barn at Thomaston are crammed with items. As I walk around the warehouse, I see objects that are a) beautiful, b) seriously old, c) and genuinely unusual. I walk around carefully, as though I were in an eclectic museum, trying not to bump into any thing or any person. I try to take notes, remember particular pieces, but there are so many it is hard to do; one thousand objects will be sold during the two days. Besides, I'm not buying, not at this auction, not in this crowd. Most everyone is in their late 50s, 60s, and older, with a smattering of younger people, mostly accompanying their grandparents and great-grandparents. My first thought is "summer people" although perhaps not; perhaps many of them are the retirees who occupy—like a pleasant, invading army—the coast.

In any case, the crowd looks like money. This is a Saturday, in a barn on the coast of Maine, so the crowd is dressed casually, but it isn't soiled t-shirts and ragged jeans casual; it is fleece vests, salmon-colored polo shirts, topsiders, LL Bean. I see one tank-top in the crowd, and there are no tattoos or body-piercings, except for diamond and gold earrings for women. There are more blonds than Maine could possibly produce. All of the men look like Walter Cronkite. Even the few people in t-shirts seem to be monied. Several couples strike me as odd: middle-aged men, rather nondescript, with stunning, younger women. In Maine you don't see this arrangement very often.

Only a few auction houses use computers to track customers; Thomaston is one of them. Theirs is a very sophisticated operation, which registers you and your license and credit card information, after which they give you your buyer's card—a stiff piece of cardboard with your number on it. I used to think the auctioneers reused these cards, and I would carefully return mine at the end of each auction, but then realized this obviously wasn't the case. Now they become bookmarks, or places for notes. Many in the audience will write down prices on the back of the card; some cards even have places for such note-taking printed on the back.

Whichever auction house it is, someone with good handwriting is in charge of the numbers—they are always written in broad, felt-tip pen, and beautifully and perfectly done. Being able to read the numbers is crucial, of course, for the auctioneer, though I have several times seen people simply shout out their number when they've stuffed a number into a pocket somewhere and can't find it, and auctioneers usually accept this informality.

About half of Thomaston Place is filled with folding seats, wooden seats, in rows, but rather loosely in rows—even here, at this upscale auction, some of the inherent casualness of a Maine auction has been preserved. Many of the seats have cushions on them, almost all have a sheet of paper with a name written on it, claiming the spot. At 11 a.m., when the auction is to begin, the seats are half-filled, people still milling among the auction items.

But gradually people flow from one side of the building to the other, wriggling in to their seats past the already seated.

There is a doorway halfway back in the audience side of the hall, leading outside, to where the obligatory food stand has been set up underneath a circus tent. Hot dogs are still on the menu, but you can also get chowders, vegetarian food, weird stuff. Single males tend to cluster in the doorway, neither part of the auction nor divorced from it. This is where I stand, since I don't intend to bid. A video person has a seat in front of the outside door, where she is beaming an image to several tv monitors scattered along the edges of the audience's end of the hall. This, and the catalogue, ensures that the buyers have a clear image of what they are being invited to bid on—both an aid and a marketing device.

Finally, everyone has settled into their seats—or almost everyone, as there will always be a few stragglers still inspecting items to be brought up, and people who get up mid-auction to check out something that caught their eye in the catalogue but which hasn't yet been sold.

The auctioneer comes to his lectern, set to one side of the main aisle so that the runners can hold up items to his right, our left, on the other side of the aisle. "All right everyone, we're going to get started," he says. The auctioneer is Kaja Veiullex. He is 57, a French-Canadian native of Waterville, who has thick black hair that swoops back from his forehead and which he occasionally runs his hand through from front to back, as people with thick black hair often do. He is wearing a white and blue-striped shirt and chinos, which already distinguishes him from every other auctioneer I've ever seen in Maine.

"I hope today's auction will be amusing, entertaining," he says, by way of introduction. "We have a _wonderful_ group of beautiful, fascinating items." He offers a few more introductory remarks, and then launches in.

The first item is a little metal bird, about four inches tall, whose purpose I can't discern. But apparently someone can, as bids come in quickly and in seconds the bird has been dispatched for $3300, more than any item has ever sold at any of the dozens and dozens of other auctions I've been to.

This is a shock. It is a little like venturing into an unfamiliar restaurant and opening the menu, and realizing you can't afford to eat there.

I keep my hand and bidding card very low, so that I don't accidentally bid on something I can't afford. This is only partially a joke: I once saw bidding for a beautiful, huge, old braided rug go vigorously back and forth at Clyde Allen's auction house, from $300 to $325 to $350, where it ended, and a short time later one of the runners came up to the stage, whispered something in Clyde's ear and he folded over, put his hands on his knees and shook his head disgustedly, then looked up and said, "Folks, we're going to have to resell that rug from a bit ago—the lady thought 'three fifty' was three dollars and fifty cents." The room exploded in laughter, and Clyde grudgingly laughed along. I didn't see who the woman was; she had probably fled right away, fearing the humiliation of the auction, which is a very real thing.

Bidding is a very public activity. All eyes turn to the person who has made a bid. A number is proposed by the auctioneer, a hand goes up, everyone turns to that hand, and then another hand goes up and we look that way, and if a third hand goes up we follow it. If there are just two, the crowd watches avidly. When the bidding goes on and on, we swivel back and forth like at a tennis match, and even though the bidding might take only 30 seconds, if it goes beyond a few back and forths, the crowd tenses, senses the drama, the battle, until it is finally resolved, and the energy of the audience is released.

Usually there are no bidders at first, until the auctioneer works his price down, to the point where someone is willing to weigh in. My guess is that the price where someone lifts a hand is almost arbitrary; that is, I doubt most of us at an auction have any plan for our bidding. We just know we don't want _that_ thing at <u>that</u> price, and then a magic number pops up and the hand goes up. The strategizing, the planning, comes in knowing what you won't go <u>beyond</u>. When my wife and I go to auctions, and see a piece we like, we will usually agree on a place to stop, an upper limit, but not on a number where we'll start.

Here in Thomaston the unfolding drama has a different arc. Kaja proposes a number, and rarely does he have to drop much below that number to get bidding going. Over the years I've noticed that most auctioneers (although not all—see below) start with the number they think the object will end up selling for, but Kaja seems to begin at a true starting point. Kaja is also quick. Almost every item is dealt with in under 30 seconds; I timed him. Since he will try to work his way through 500 items on this lovely Saturday, that's more than four hours of auctioneering, so it pays to be quick.

Auctioneers have several catch phrases, which they use at different parts of the bidding process. Kaja's most distinctive one comes when he is about to end the bidding, as he waves his hand above his head, over the audience, like a conductor preparing to conclude the final held note: "All in, all done?" he'll say, then point dramatically at the winner. Later, in mid-winter, I ask him where he got this refrain from: "I don't know. I do that, really?" he asks, puzzled that he is so consistent with it.

Another of his refrains, which seems so self-consciously disingenuous that I assume he knows it, is when he introduces a piece, and says with enthusiasm, "the finest one we've ever had in the building." One supposes this could technically be true, in the sense that this particular piece has never been in the building, even though there may have been others exactly like it, but not—existentially speaking—this one. Again I ask, and Kaja says, "No, that's true. We know everything about the piece, and we guarantee it. If I say it's the finest one we've ever had, then I know that's true."

The flow of an auction can be hypnotic as the item comes up, Kaja describes it, launches in, and the "All in, all done?" tolls and the final summary sounds, "Sold! to number 59 for forty-nine hundred dollars," and then starts up again. But there are moments when the flow stops, when something out of the ordinary happens.

Kaja's auction has a long table at the back of the hall, where about half a dozen well-dressed employees of the House sit, each with either a phone or a computer or both in front of him or her. I had no idea what these people were doing until the first day of the Thomaston auction was well-launched. It turns out they are representing off-site bidders, who have registered beforehand and are called when the item they are interested in comes up, or who will follow along on a computer and bid via the Thomaston Place employee, or will have placed an absentee bid, which the employee will represent, by standing up from the table, phone at the ear, and shouts out a bid.

On the Saturday sale two off-site bidders were being represented by the phone bank at the back of the hall. A tall grey-haired man, Bob Grant, stood and shouted out "five hundred" and Kaja repeated the number, but before he could move into his chant of "five hundred, I have five hundred, do I hear five fifty?" another off-site person rose and shouted out "six hundred." Then the first one responded with "seven hundred" and back and forth it went, no one else in the hall bidding, Kaja entirely left out, and up front he shrugged and reached for some water and leaned against the podium, while the audience burst into laughter at this unusual sight. This went on for almost a minute, and finally Bob Grant got it for his bidder. Then Kaja put down his water and went back to work.

Another variation on the formula comes when there is a particularly lively contest between two or more bidders, who won't give up. Somehow it is better if there are just two; while it is often the case that one person gets the bidding going, and another person joins in, and then a third, and a bidder can drop out temporarily and re-enter later and still claim the prize, there is much more drama if there are only two, and the bidding goes back and forth between those two for a long time—"long" in auction terms being more than a minute.

The item being coveted was a combination knife-pistol from 1830, and the bidding ping-ponged from one side of the room to the other (it's even better if there is that clear distance between the bidders; the bidding war where one person is sitting in front of another is hard to follow, and loses some of its dramatic value), until finally the bidder on the far side of the hall, a man, turned and looked at his wife, which is a sign of defeat. Almost always when the person turns to his or her spouse, partner, lover, accountant, that person is done. He/she is looking for some guidance, some support from the other person, but if you need that support—especially at the level of a Kaja auction—you're probably all in and all done. Someone else took the curious-looking knife-pistol for $11,000.

One of the many new things I hadn't encountered before I came to Thomaston, was the tradition of showing appreciation for a particularly dramatic sale through applause. The most dramatic moment of the two days takes place about midway through day one of the 2008 auction, when item #100 comes up, an "OOC" (oil on canvas, in the vernacular) called "Roman Newsboys II," by Martin Johnson Heade, a painter I'd never heard of—no particular surprise there—from the late 19th century. This obviously is the signature piece of the sale, featured on the back cover of the auction catalogue, and with a very long description. The estimates on it were from $150,000 to $200,000, by far the highest number for anything in the catalogue.

The bidding began and at first I didn't pay much attention, not being particularly smitten by the painting and having left my one hundred thousand dollar bills at home, but when the bidding reached $200,000 I looked around to see who was involved. There was someone bidding by phone, and one person in the crowd, whose gestures were so subtle that for the longest time I couldn't tell who it was. Other people in the hall were turned toward the back of the hall, and I could find the bidder only because eventually everyone was glancing in the same direction. The bidder was a rough-looking old boy I hadn't noticed before, in ragged shorts and a polo shirt, extremely casual among this crowd of pastels and pearls.

The bidding proceeded in $25,000 increments, from $200,000 to $225,000 to $250,000. There were no pauses of the sort you get when someone is deciding. This was swift, assured bidding, until we got to $400,000, then there was a pause. But our man never wavered, and finally it was his at $475,000. That got a sustained round of applause. The rough fellow, tipped back in his chair on its rear legs with his feet on the chair in front, smiled slightly in acknowledgement and that was all.

"People come to Maine to buy antiques and art objects because of the moral attitudes of the people selling it," Kaja tells me, speaking precisely, as though he is articulating an important principle. "They want to buy in Maine because of that assumption about how we are."

We are sitting at a table inside of Thomaston Place on the first of February, when I was expecting the showroom would be empty, silent; instead, there is a bustle of activity, as this is "free appraisal day," and a steady flow of people walk out the doors, carrying a baffling variety of items. "I've been doing this one day a week for forty years," Kaja says as we watch the parade. Anyone can bring in an object, and Kaja or his business partner John Botero, or the chief researcher, Dave Fletcher, will tell them what they know about it, and how much it might be worth. An "Antiques Road Show," except stationary.

I asked why, at his auctions, he always tells which house an object came from, naming the town, telling a little bit about the person who owned it.

"The auctioneer's job is to educate and entertain," Kaja says. "You watch: some other places just describe the item, no information other than 'This is a clock made in 1925.' I tell the background of the piece, where it came from—the mystique of where things come from adds twenty to fifty percent to the sale price."

Kaja's family is French Canadian, from Quebec and Prince Edward Island, and his father finished only the 8th grade, but was "a genius with numbers. He could do math in his head exceptionally well, and some of that got passed on to me." His family had a grocery store in Waterille—Veilleux meat-markets, where Kaja worked, from the ages of eight to fifteen (it's a little hard to picture this man who travels in expensive circles, selling items worth hundreds of thousands of dollars, wearing, now, a black topcoat with a red vest, dramatic colors, chopping meat), and his father was in construction, and bought up whole houses to sell in pieces as well. "Which is how I got into it. I was programmed for trading. I've been trading since I was eight. My ancestors were pack rats, which was passed on to me. And I've got a passion for preservation. After high school [in Waterville] I worked as a framer in downtown Waterville, at Berry's Stationery, from fifteen to twenty, so that probably has something to do with it. You know, I'd never been inside an art museum until I was 18?

"I've got one hundred percent photographic recall—I can tell you exactly what an item sold for, no matter how many years ago, and I can tell you everything about it, too. It just sticks in my head. It drives my wife crazy. I'll be sitting watching television in the evening, flipping through antiques catalogues and I'll be able to remember every piece I saw in the catalogue, while the show is on."

I test him on this ability with a strange looking object I inherited from my Grandmother nearly twenty years ago. I describe it for him: a container in the shape of a skull, with a snake winding in and out of the eye holes. "Oh, those are German," Kaja replies instantly, "a stein. There's also a humidor made in that fashion, Japanese I think. Wooden, but some are ceramic. And there's a frog on top, right?" That's exactly so, down to the frog on top of the lid. He tells me the price it might get, but I'm so discouraged to discover it isn't worth thousands I don't bother writing the number down.

Kaja got his start doing household auctions in Waterville, "standing in the doorway of a house, selling off everything inside to people standing in the yard. I used to do as many as sixty-eight auctions like that in a year."

Now he has entered a rarified air in Thomaston, running four multi-day fine art auctions each year, and more if he can find the right merchandise. His crew is hoping to pull together enough items for a two-day sale in late May, but "we've got to sell more than a million dollars worth, or we lose money," he tells me. "The overhead on this operation is brutal. Our profit margin is only two percent. We spend fifty thousand dollars for the brochures and flyers for each sale. They go all over. We advertise in London newspapers and in the Newtown Bee in Connecticut, in the antique journals, in targeted journals, we print thousands of catalogues—we'll pay to place 15 photos, say, of select items for the European or international market. We'll get calls from Russia—got a call recently on a jade knife that we bought for one hundred-eighty five at a little shop near here, and it sold for twelve thousand."

Each auction requires about one thousand hours of preparation on the part of the Thomaston Place crew, and each piece is worth $255 in overhead; in other words, any piece that doesn't clear $255 is a loss. "We put up a lot of money in restoration. Ten thousand to restore a painting sometimes."

I've always wondered how an auctioneer works a crowd, what the tricks are, aside from the obvious need to remember where you are in the bidding, and whose bid is whose. One is that "The opening sets the tone for the day, so you want to have good stuff at the start." What about knowing what number to begin with? Does he have a sheet with that number on it next to the item? Does he prepare beforehand for that all-important starting point? "Nope," he says, shaking his head. "I pick the number out of the air—it's not written down." What about deciding on the increments from one ask to the next? It turns out there are rules about this: "Once you establish an increment, like a hundred dollars, say, you have to stick with it." He also says that sales are controlled to some degree by the fact that sometimes there is a "reserve" on an item—in other words, a minimum that the owner says he or she won't accept less than (except when Kaja owns the piece, in which case he has his own sense of what he will or won't sell it for), and another protection, in that if an item doesn't "open on the floor," then he'll "pass" it. I'd always thought that in an auction you had to sell every item, and had to accept any bid, but apparently this isn't so: "At a country auction, or a liquidation, everything does sell, but in a gallery auction that's not the case. Items have reserves that I can't go below, and the auctioneer's number one priority is to protect our clients. Even if we would collect a commission on a sale, we can't go below what the piece is worth, and have our clients not get a fair sale."

He tells me of one other complication I never would have thought of. "I have to be sure to have plenty of good things on the Sunday sale, for the Jewish buyers—they can't come on Saturday, naturally, so Sunday can't be dreck."

I ask about the sale the previous year of the Heade painting, sold to the big fellow. Of course he remembers the sale; he remembers every sale. I had wondered afterwards if perhaps that man had been buying for someone else. Kaja shakes his head. "No, I know him very well. He's a Texan. He was buying for himself. I think he takes that painting back and forth, from his Texas place, then up here during the summer."

He knows many of the other auctioneers in the state. I mention Clyde Allen and he says, "Oh, Clyde was great—what a voice, and always rolled up his sleeves," which is exactly what you would remember about Clyde if you'd seen him in action. He tells a story about another auctioneer, a notoriously crude one, Tiny Bill, who, naturally, was enormously fat and swore at everyone, but was very effective as an auctioneer.

He is particularly enthusiastic about an item that is coming up in his May auction: the original draft of Ralph Waldo Emerson's poem, "Concord Hymn," read at the Concord battleground commemoration in 1837, which includes the famous line, "The Shot Heard Round the World." "It's the draft he carried with him to the reading," Kaja says, marveling once again, at all the special objects there are in the world.

I tell him he must be exhausted at the end of his sales. "Not a bit," he says, "I love it—I could go on all day. I love what I do. I have people, computer people, people with a lot of money, tell me, 'I would love to do what you do.' I get to spend most of my day with beautiful objects. What could be better?"

In between Rome and Thomaston, both physically and economically, are many other auctions and auction houses; in this zone the differences between one place and another become incremental rather than continental. At least three auction houses sit in this zone: Clyde Allen's in New Sharon, Holmes Auction Center in Skowhegan, and Houston & Brooks in Burnham. Clyde's has been around for years, since the 60s, and the Clyde of the title, Clyde Allen, is an icon in the area, the first auctioneer I ever heard in action, and still one of the most distinctive; although, one of the discoveries one makes when one is a serial-auction attender is that all auctioneers have a style, a manner about them. If they don't have such a flair, they don't last—no one wants to hear them or see them, for they turn the auction from entertainment into drudgery.

Clyde was a trim man with a booming voice. He always wore tight jeans with a big belt buckle, a cowboy shirt with the arms rolled up, and cowboy boots, and he could really roar. He never used a microphone, and he had the least patience of any auction-eer I've seen for when the noise in the hall got too loud. This is another one of those measures of an auctioneer, how they re-spond to crowd noise. Clyde used to shout, "Quiet down please! You're going to have to quiet down!" and the hubbub would drop for a bit, then bubble back up slowly. Sometimes he would get so mad his face would turn red and the veins in his neck stand out. Sadly, he had a stroke one day and his son Rodney took over. Rod-ney uses a microphone. "I had a herniated disc, and I found out that the louder I hollered the more that disc hurt, I'll tell you."

Harold never admonishes the crowd, perhaps because his auction is pure entertainment, and the louder it is the more fun people are having. Kaja is, fittingly, the most genteel about it: he whispers, "shh, shh" through his microphone and that's it. No commands to shut up, no calls to quiet down, a simple shushing.

Clyde's auction house is off Industry Road in New Sharon, two left hand turns from Route Two if one is headed east. Clyde built it about 1974 just for his auction business. The building is set back from the road in a broad field, which is all mud during the spring and summer rains. A stage is raised on the eastern end of the hall, the snack bar in one corner of the west end, the auc-tion office in the other corner, separated by the bathrooms. The chairs have pads on them that the audience brings, and many of the chairs are claimed by boxes with newspaper inside, for wrap-ping up the glassware the owner is hoping to buy. There are two garage doors across from each other just in front of the stage, on either side of the building. On a nice early summer evening, the garage door to the south is sometimes left open and golden evening light and the sweet air streams in, and the hall becomes both auction and front porch.

Clyde's son, Rodney, who does snow plowing, logging, "some appraising," during the off-season, has taken over for Clyde, who still comes to the auctions, perched in the back corner by the snack bar, sitting on his walker. At an auction a few years ago, a large American flag comes up for sale, with 48 stars. "Don't touch it to the floor boys," Rodney says respectfully. Almost everything is subject to humor at auctions—women especially, but also fellow auctioneers, children, the audience, even the items themselves—but one thing never joked about is the flag or patriotism. Even in the auction house, patriotism is sacred.

Later, Rodney brings up a zebra skin rug. I think it's fantastic; Rodney jokes, "You'll be the only one to have something like it," he says, which gets a huge, derisive laugh. He starts the bidding low, so I know he's not expecting much. Besides, it's probably illegal to own an exotic animal skin in Maine. I buy it for $35; later that year I happen to be in South Africa, and I see one exactly like it, except newer, hanging on the wall of an upscale African Arts shop on the waterfront in Cape Town. The price? 14,000 Rand, or about two thousand dollars. I win.

For some reason the auctioneers at Clyde's have always pronounced Japan as "Jap-an" with equal stress on both syllables. And everything is "she" as in "she's in pretty good shape." If something is basically and truly junk then it's "not that bad." Rodney brings up an old toy bicycle that is falling apart and says, "You got a grandkid you don't like, this is the toy you want," to laughter, although he's tapped into a truth, which is that many of the items at Clyde's would make good Christmas gifts, in the right family. And most of the collection here couldn't possibly be found in a store.

Rodney's assistant takes over, a janitor in a nearby school with a reedy voice who is more sing-songy in his approach. He uses the refrain "three dollar bill" a lot, as in "two dollar, two dollar, who'll give me a three dollar bill." Clyde's is the kind of place where the helpers will yelp if they see a hand go up that they don't think Rodney has seen. This can be a jolting noise, nearly a shriek, and I'm never sure if Rodney appreciates the assistance.

A kneeler from a church goes for $22.50, a used punching bag (used for jokes, at this auction) for $57.50, a Sawyer print for $45 (seems low). I notice a state Senator in the crowd, wearing a baseball cap with his name and title monogrammed on it. A lawn tractor with some years on it is for sale, and they open one of the garage doors and make a big show of driving it in, out of control, since the helper isn't sure how to operate it, which gets applause from the amused audience, appreciating the spectacle, the entertainment of it all. But still, the lawn tractor doesn't sell.

I went to my first Harold Holmes Auction Center auction right after Labor Day, on a Thursday morning, when this Harold always holds his auctions. Which prompts one to wonder what the reason would be to hold an auction on a Thursday morning? What is the strategy? (Harold tells me later, "There is no right day. They'd come at 1 a.m. on a Sunday morning if you held it then.") The audience was sure to be older on a Thursday morning, as everyone younger was either at work or in school or in diapers.

Most auctions—actually, all auctions—attract older crowds. Perhaps this isn't so surprising: older people have the money and the leisure to attend auctions, and in addition they have an interest in the kinds of things that are offered in Maine—in old stuff, in kitsch, in antiques, in things that speak of Maine, in items that remind them of being young, of childhood, of kids who are no longer kids. That kind of stuff. You rarely see young people at an auction, unless they are pre-teen children, and then they're bored, restless, or playing on Game Boys or listening to ipods. It does make one wonder about the future of the country auction, about whether the next several generations will value this form of entertainment, these types of items.

As always, there is an office, a snack bar, and otherwise a big open room, about the same size as Clyde's, but newer. One odd aspect of this sale was that two auctioneers took turns, back and forth. One was the eponymous "Harold Holmes" the owner, but for the most part the two split the calling duties. "Takes the heat off," Holmes says. The auctioneers, Harold and Rob, rarely chastise about noise ("Do you like being yelled at?" Holmes asks me. "I don't either, so I don't yell."). They eschew microphones, too, perhaps because of the cement floor that reflects their voices, and the relatively small size of the audience, which tends to stay seated, not milling and chatting. Plus, Harold has a good auctioneer's voice, firm but not too penetrating; Rob's voice is higher yet distinctive. Harold was fast and emphatic, and had the habit of being chagrined, tortured even, when he ended the sale and realized he'd missed a bid—that someone had lifted his or her hand just as he called the end (and contrary to the popular image, auctioneers rarely, if ever, use the phrase "going once, going twice . . ."). He would bunch his fist, bow his head, and clench as though in pain, and say, "God damn it I missed it, I missed it. I'm sorry. People, you got to raise your hands sooner." I wasn't sure if he was mad at himself or at the bidder. Rob always begins at something like, "give me a hundred dollars, a hundred dollars," but doesn't turn to face the audience until he's dropped to a more reasonable number; doing so, he gives it away that "one hundred" is not a serious ask.

The merchandise is similar to but probably a bit more interesting and valuable than at Clyde's, with a few gems sprinkled in. A blanket chest comes up that has "Maine 1846" made out of thin birch branches on the front, and the whole thing seems to have been made out of split birch. Of course, when I buy it, it turns out to be birch bark over plywood, and not made in 1846 at all, but it's still kind of charming.

As with the other Harold's auction, it isn't always possible to tell which items were for sale and which were part of the permanent décor. A large, bad painting on the east wall of the building catches my eye. It shows two hunters dragging a deer through snow back to a cabin in the woods. It is a rather lurid painting, badly done, but it has a sort of rough, country charm. I don't want to own it, but I want to know who <u>would</u> want to. But it never comes up for sale; not the first time, and not the next two times I am in attendance either.

I learned a new phrase at this auction, which was "architectural item," the term used by Rob for anything that he couldn't identify. A post of no particular character appears and it becomes an "architectural item" because he's not sure if it's a bed post or a porch post, or a railing or what. People smile, knowing what he means, probably sharing his puzzlement. Rob also likes the term "aggravation" as "there's some aggravation to the handle" of the bean pot he's holding, meaning it is damaged. "Aggravation" is a lot more appealing than "broken." Among the oddities at the sale this day are a molasses pump (a long tube for pumping molasses out of a barrel, which itself would have to be for sale in order for the pump to be useful); a big box of *Galaxy* magazines, a science fiction magazine from the 50s and 60s, which sells for $75; an oddly shaped trumpet, and a perfectly nice couch that doesn't sell, even at the final asking price of one dollar.

I ask Harold about his sales, how he would characterize them. "I'm a generalist," he says. "Every auction is different because we've always got different material. The merchandise dictates what kind of sale it is. We're a country auction, that's what you'd call us." I agree that "country auction" would be a good name for his and the other mid-range auctions in the state. Holmes adds a nice qualifier that sums the issue of definition very well: "Ultimately," he says, "you are what you sell."

One Thursday I count baseball hats being worn in the audience. There are 30, out of a total of 60 people. A fellow standing beside me at the rear of the hall buys a glass-headed cane, a trombone (I ask him if he plays; he says no), and a 45-recording of George Harrison singing a forgotten ditty, "Apple Scruffs." I ask my neighbor what he's going to do with this eclectic lot. He'll sell it on eBay is the unsurprising and disappointing answer. Somehow I was hoping that this odd group of things meant something important to him, revealed an essential truth about him, but I guess not.

Towards the end of the auction, several hours in, when the auctioneers and the audience are both tired, Holmes starts to zip through items. He races so fast through the final items that the recorder who sits at his feet all throughout the auction can't keep up. He gets through his description, the low-ball price ("two dollars, who'll give me two dollars?"), and the quick sale—the first hand up—before she can write down the lot number, the item description, and the sale price. We are on the verge of chaos.

"It's exhausting," Holmes tells me later. "After all, you're performing, and for three, four hours, however long the auction lasts. But it's fun. The rest of the week is work, but auction day is fun."

Houston-Brooks is a strange auction; not as strange as Harold's in Rome, but strange. Their auctions are held on Sunday mornings, which is already strange; and they start at 7am, which is really odd. Their building is outside the town of Burnham (Burnham is a town that is all "outside"—there is no inside to it that I can find) on a lonely road, South Horseback Road (does a town the size of Burnham really need to distinguish between the North and South versions of Horseback Road?).

The main building, close to the road, was a grange hall at one time, and was moved a short ways from the corner of South Horseback and the Troy Road to this spot for reasons involving noisy grange hall dances and a testy widow. Behind it and beneath it is a wide barn with four bays, though it's not really a barn, more like a shed constructed for the purpose of the auction. The barn auction is the one that starts at 7, and when that one concludes, and after a short pause, the 11 a.m. auction begins in the church/main building, which is graced with a sign that says, "We Buy Junk. We Sell Antiques."

Each sale has its own auctioneer. The barn auction is run by Danny Brooks, who is a fast-moving auctioneer. He is in the "quiet-them-down" camp, and from time to time on his queer perch (a cart that can be wheeled around, on to which he climbs, with his headset and his clipboard, like a moveable altar and he's the priest) he will shout for people to "Quiet down, please, quiet down." The barn auction has furniture and tools, big items and quirky items, like a wooden Doctor's examining table, the ugliest bed frame I've ever seen, Ellwood typewriter oil, ivory elephant carvings.

Houston-Brooks has the most ambitious food of any auction house I frequent. It is almost a café, with the regular food counter and three or four square, café-esque tables set in front, beyond the display area for the auction. Between the lower and the upper auctions people flock here, for breakfast, lunch, coffee, and some loiter even while the 11 o'clock sale starts.

The auctioneer in the old grange hall above at 11 is Shane, the tall son of Pam and Danny Brooks, who uses crutches sometimes because of Multiple Sclerosis. He makes his way to the head of the room after the lower sale ends, nearly 11:30, and takes his place on a platform, behind a counter. He pulls on his headset for the sound system, then delivers the usual preamble about the rules of the auction, which are also printed on a poster on a wall. Every auction has its own rules, along with the state-required ones. They are supposed to be announced before the sale begins, and sometimes are. Here, the rules are a 12% premium on sales, minus 2% for cash or check payment; no sales tax for dealers who can show their tax-exempt status. This complicates the bidding when you have to calculate your bid plus 10%, or 15.5%, if you account for the sales tax. No one does.

Shane is genial and thanks people for their bids. He is fast, and the merchandise up here is of an entirely different character than that below. More "art," more curiosities here, and no furniture. You see things you could never see anywhere else, and you have never seen before. There is a Buckley's Hygenic Hair Drier, which is a metal piece with a horn on top, like the speaker of an old Victorola, and a bottom container that holds some sort of fluid which is ignited and sends out a flame from the horn, which is then used for drying hair. It goes for $75, so someone must see the value of it.

Some Nazi memorabilia comes up, a helmet and flag, and I imagine I can feel the distaste in the room for them. The room seems to grow quieter, as we wonder (I imagine) who would buy such a thing, who would want it anywhere around him, who would even want to touch it. The helmet and flag sell quickly; there seems to be no enthusiasm for the sale, though, even on the part of Shane, who merely describes the item, sets a price, and seems to want to get rid of it as soon as possible.

The other half of the hall, the part that must have been where the wallflowers at a grange dance gathered, is where the people like me wander, leaning against pillars, fingering some of the items that will be sold at the last, the low-end items, usually. At a sale in mid-winter, under one of those classic slate-grey winter skies, the collection shows signs of fatigue, almost desperation. There is a fishing reel, and a Mickey Mouse hand puppet, and a ceramic napkin holder in the shape of a baseball glove with a baseball forever embedded in the palm of the glove. In other words, we may have crossed over from auction to yard sale. But it is winter, everything in Maine is tired, and by spring the offerings will revive, one hopes.

Houston-Brooks sells more guns than other auctions do, which fits nicely with the many animal heads displayed high on the walls all around the hall; again, like all objects placed high at every auction house, they are not actually for sale. The stuffed martin, bear, caribou rack, deer, will be here the next time I come, and the time after that.

Pam Brooks has no illusions about where their auction falls on the scale in Maine, or who they are, as defined by what they sell, to borrow Harold Holmes' succinct phrase. "The niche we're in, is mediocre stuff—we're middle of the road. I'm not saying our stuff is bad, but because we sell what comes through the door we don't have the high end things. Ninety percent is brought to us; only about ten percent is material we went out and found. If we get it on a Monday, chances are we're selling it on Sunday. We don't have the storage to keep things and arrange sales around particular themes." Yet, they still attract buyers from all over. "Oh yes, we pull from all up and down the east coast, from Texas in the summer, Canadians . . . they're a mix—retailers, collectors, people who are bored."

For years I've tried to figure out what the logic in the ordering of items is. Sometimes it seems the tiny items, the glass-ware or flatware, goes first, at excruciating length. Certainly this is the way it is at Clyde's, where the glass-front display case of such items is drained first, and then the dishes on top or on the side tables. Aside from that pattern, my guess is that there is a crescendo aimed for about midway, when the most desired items comes up. Kaja told me, aside from whatever strategy he uses, the first half hour gets the most money.

"The opening sets the tone for the day," he said in February. "Lots of auctioneers start with the cheap stuff—I think that's a mistake. But you have to have variety, too, so that people don't move—you make it so they don't want to move, because they might miss something. So you can't have all high end or all low end. I try to arrange the sale so that every 5 or 10 or 15 items there is a high point, something exciting."

Harold Holmes says "The best stuff first," but they don't usually organize their auctions with an official "Order of Auction" has Kaja does. Kaja's auctions are so organized that the items are arranged in order in the catalogue, which of course has to be printed well ahead of the auction. Rodney Allen agrees that "the best stuff goes first, down to the box lots" but adds that he tries to stick to one lot at a time, "otherwise it's awfully hard on my mother," who is the recorder at most of his auctions, to keep track of.

I wonder about the psychology of the auction, too. When someone bids on something, anything, it makes me want to spend money, even if I don't particularly want that thing. I suppose it's like being in a casino: seeing other people spend money makes you want to spend money. The auctioneer makes a joke and we all laugh, and it's just a pleasure to see the stuff paraded before you. And as it passes, to some degree you desire it, and when you don't get it, the frustration builds a little, and you want it more. It's a strange form of avarice that surfaces at an auction.

The sheer volume of items for sale at Holmes and at Houston-Brooks and Clyde's raises the obvious question: where do they get all this stuff? Where does all of it come from? How many old pieces of nebulous value are out there? Does it just show up, do they have an army of hunter-gatherers out there removing the possessions of Maine's citizens?

Holmes in Skowhegan says he gets his items from all over, including Canada and New Brunswick. "We get referrals, word of mouth. People call up, they show up—we're here seven days a week—and sometimes we travel out to get things. Most of my audience is dealers, some collectors." Pam Brooks mostly receives; rarely do they seek. "It comes in, it goes out, we have to do it that way." Rodney Allen also is on the receiving end: "My Dad had a good reputation, so people come to us. Sometimes someone will call us up and I'll go look at a house."

As with everything else, Thomaston is the outlier. Thomaston employs a full-time crew of people to seek out high-end items, which must be daunting work, since, given the level at which Kaja operates, it won't do to have low quality goods at their sale. Thomaston also has Dave Fletcher, who is the researcher behind the operation. You see him at auctions, wandering around at the front in his black leather vest, black jeans, behind and sometimes in front of Kaja, looking for something but it's not clear what. Perhaps it is a continuation of what he does the rest of the year, when he burrows through homes, identifying riches, researching the detritus of a life that is offered to him, or which he comes across, surprised. Even here, Kaja and his crew are often recipients rather than recruiters: the free appraisal days bring in many pieces that will end up in a sale. But Kaja makes far more house calls than other Maine auction houses, and Thomaston's research department makes a huge difference in who sells through them, as "we are hired to be the brains to help liquidate a family's belongings. Like a highboy that once belonged to John Adams, that I saw recently."

The end result of all this effort in Thomaston is to put one in awe of how many gorgeous, old, precious objects are still lurking in closets and attics and mud rooms throughout New England. One would have thought the storehouse of riches would have been exhausted by now, but apparently not. Still, over the last two decades, one can see the desiccation, the deterioration in the riches of Maine, at least at my local auction house. I have friends whose lovely dining room furnishings were supplied by Clyde's auctions. But Clyde's doesn't have such riches anymore; it isn't the fault of Clyde, or Rodney, it is a function of what is available now in their area. As Rodney says of the stock that makes up his sales, "It's going down on my end. Older dealers are going out of business, and new shops don't have the interest, at least in antiques. Antique prices aren't bringing what they did; I'll bet they're down fifty percent from what they were."

One snapshot of the changes: in the two decades I have been going to Clyde's auctions, I've gone from bidding on items for our house, to only seeing things I'd want for our camp. Nothing wrong with them, but they fit a camp, not a house.

Ultimately an auction in Maine is supposed to be fun; thrilling even. One might end up buying something one doesn't want, and is horrified to now own, but it is the chase that is interesting, unless—like the big fellow in Thomaston—you're bidding four hundred and seventy-five thousand dollars; then it must be terrifying.

Kaja tells a story that captures the fairy tale hope that lurks in the hearts of everyone involved with auctions. It starts with a horse blanket.

"A picker [a fellow who goes around looking for items, sometimes called a 'scout'] bought an old Larkin desk or something like that, from a lady in Skowhegan. He needed something to protect it, and the lady said 'You can have this old horse blanket.' The guy gave her two dollars for it. Another picker bought it from him for a hundred bucks, because that second guy knew it was a bed blanket, not a horse blanket, and I bought it from him for twenty-five hundred dollars, and I sold it to another guy in New Hampshire the next day for ten thousand dollars. So in less than twenty-four hours it had passed through four hands, from two dollars to ten thousand. And not long after it was bought in Skowhegan for two dollars, it was being offered for sale in New York for $50,000. It was a big, thick bed blanket that had been made by Longfellow's great-grandmother in about 1770."

Back at Harold's on the penultimate Saturday night of the season, the crowd is sparse and the garage is cold. The garage door is locked, and the front door is closed quickly after anyone enters or exits. Bidding is slow, sometimes absent altogether, until Harold adjusts to the mood of the crowd and drops his asking prices lower and lower, where he's asking a dollar, or saying "First hand gets it for two dollars," then "sold!" he shouts as the first hand lifts. Brick holds up a "Betty Boop cookie jar," which seems precious and desirable among the nondescript and utterly ordinary household items that are on offer. Still, people are having a good time, and Brick is still bantering with Harold or with the audience, and as time wears on Harold gets more and more flippant. "That other one was a piece of shit," he says when the second of two table lamps, identical to one another, comes up for bid. The crowd laughs, and Harold, observing the conventions of dry wit, doesn't crack a smile. He pretends a set of dishes were "my own sainted mother's," heaving with sobs as he says this, then sells them quickly and waves them away. I don't know if he's trying for humor when he starts the bidding on an extremely ordinary, if not ugly, floor lamp by saying "That's got a three way switch," drawing out each word of "three way switch" as though a three-way switch is something special to behold.

The bidding gets lower and lower, the objects lifted up more and more dreary—one gets the feeling that a runner might have just dashed out to his car and grabbed whatever was there—but still 20 or so people stay, and they still buy. We are nearly at the point where Harold is giving items away, the whole thing is about to fold up, and Harold is crooning, "It's Saturday night, folks, it's auction night," almost to himself.

Carrots

(2014)

I was pulling up the last of the carrots from my garden when I heard my neighbor's pickup truck turn into his driveway, a hundred yards up hill from our house. I was still wearing the hunter orange jacket I'd had on when I took the dog out for a walk in a large open field a few miles away. I pulled up a few large carrots, scraped some of the mud and a bit of ice off them—it was deer season, early November, the ground starting to freeze—and looked up towards my neighbor's house.

I like pulling out the carrots this time of year; the ground clings to them, reluctant to let them go. I have to pull carefully, to keep from separating the green leafy tops from the vegetable itself, which would make it hard to lift them from the ground. It's a bit of sport, where I try to gauge the force I should apply steadily and firmly, so the carrot will come, but I'll not lose the top.

Another man, who was not my neighbor, had gotten out of the truck and was leaning against the bed of it, looking inside. Living here for more than 27 years has trained me in the implications of that particular gesture, so I knew that he was looking at something dead in the bed of the pickup. I walked out of my yard and up the road towards my neighbor's house. As I approached the driveway, I constructed the proper greeting in my head, one that would sound unjudgmental, as though shooting a deer was something I would enthusiastically endorse, never criticize, or that would sound as though it might come from a Mainer, but wouldn't sound as though I were an outsider trying to sound like a Mainer.

I hailed the man. "Did'ya get one?" I asked. He turned around slowly, as though he wasn't sure where the sound was coming from, then nodded. "Yep," he said.

I came up to the truck and looked inside. A young buck was laid out there, head towards the front, feet against the left-hand side of the truck bed. There was a gaping hole in the lower part of his belly, which I thought at first was where he had been shot, then realized no, he had been gutted. He had small, thin, beautifully smooth and matching antlers, and the blood still dripped from him. It must have been running out of the hole in his belly and underneath him, because I didn't see any in the truck itself, but the blood was dripping slowly from under the tailgate, forming a brilliant crimson pool between the feet of the man who wasn't my neighbor and mine.

My neighbor came out of his house, in hunter orange coat and cap. He didn't say anything; he doesn't usually say much. He came up to the bed and we all looked inside, my neighbor, me, and the man who wasn't my neighbor.

"Where'd you get him?" I asked, trying again to capture the sound of someone without judgment.

"Over in Farmington," my neighbor said.

"Really?" I said. "Where can you hunt there?"

"Behind the high school." The local high school sits on the top of a ridge with a grand view facing northwest, towards Quebec. There are woods to the west of the high school.

I hmphed. I am good at hmphs. "Was it a long shot?" I asked, thinking it couldn't have been, given how narrow the woods are there.

The man who wasn't my neighbor turned and pointed across the street, to a tree halfway into the apple orchard on the other side of our road. "About to there," he said, and then turned back to the deer.

"Oh, that's a pretty good shot," I said, impressed. It must have been seventy-five yards to the place he'd pointed, which seemed like a long distance for such a clean kill shot. But what did I know about it?

I was still holding the carrots in my hand. The bright green tops had not separated from the carrots and I was holding them by the greens, banging them softly against my leg. The blood dripped from beneath the tailgate, the deer was perfectly still. His antlers were small, and seemed polished almost, and utterly symmetrical with one another. The man who wasn't my neighbor stared at it.

My neighbors' wife came out of the house and joined us. She has bad arthritis and moves gingerly She looked at the deer. "Those are nice carrots you've got there," she said to me.

"Yes," I said, "I just pulled them. They're good sized."

She nodded. "You didn't take them out of my garden did you?" she asked, referring to my notoriously poor gardening skills.

"No, I got a good crop for once."

She went back inside and left us there. The man who wasn't my neighbor continued to look at the deer. He didn't have much to say. The blood dripped onto the ground. The pool was small, but brilliant in color, and it didn't soak into the ground but stayed on top, like mercury on a pane of glass.

"Where'd you hit him?" I asked, having run out of anything else to say about our situation.

My neighbor reached up high on the deer's left flank and felt around for a spot. "Right here," he said, indicating a hole on the deer's chest, near its shoulder. "Got him through the heart, I think."

I couldn't see the hole but could see where he was pointing.

It must have been a smooth, clean hole, and the deer probably died quickly, if not instantly. I didn't have any feeling for the deer as I looked at it. It was a dead deer, in the bed of a pickup. Re-markably still.

The man who wasn't my neighbor lifted one foot onto the rear bumper. I tapped my carrots against my leg. My neighbor looked at the deer. The blood ran onto the ground. My pant leg was getting muddy.

My neighbor, the deer, the blood, the man who wasn't my neighbor, the pickup.

The man who wasn't my neighbor. The carrots. The deer.

The carrots. The blood. The deer.

The deer. The carrots. The blood.

Icy Eden
(1996)

"I believe that there is a subtle magnetism in Nature . . .When I go out of the house for a walk, uncertain as yet whither I will bend my steps, and submit myself to my instinct to decide for me, . . . I finally and inevitably settle southwest . . ."—Henry David Thoreau, "Walking"

My internal compass has always pointed north, where the open spaces are; or, if not north, at least in a direction where there are fewer people than wherever "here" is. When, as a younger man, I had the leisure and wherewithal to roam, I always headed north, ending up one day on the north slope of Alaska's Brooks Range.

So it was that in February I had a great idea, and unlike most of my great ideas, this one turned out to be pretty good. I decided I would go to Bar Harbor and Acadia National Park on Mt. Desert Island, an island which dangles like an earring from Maine's coast, when no one was there, while it was empty, or as empty as it ever gets, when fewer than one percent of the year's three million visitors pass through the Park. I had already seen it in summer, had run the gauntlet of t-shirt and pizza shops and wandering crowds in Bar Harbor (the town through which nearly everyone who visits Acadia must pass), when it embodies the formula Maine + summer + coast.

I drove through the deserted streets of Bar Harbor on a Friday night, through the snow whipping across the street, out to the Bar Harbor Motor Inn on Frenchman Bay. In season, the hotel is regularly full, but on this coldest weekend of the year, I strode up to the front desk and booked a room on the first floor facing the bay.

In the morning I pulled the drapes back and the room filled with the reflected brilliance of sunrise on an empty bay. Snow had drifted against the stems of brittle weeds on the shore in scalloped swirls. A misty fog hung on the water, and above it the Porcupine Islands spread out in a bristling half circle. Behind them, on the mainland, stood Mount Battie.

Bar Harbor in winter is like any organism responding to cold: it closes in on itself, shutting down the extremities (most of the 2,500 guest rooms), keeping the community core impact. One winter several years ago, things got so quiet that the weekly police blotter was short: *Southwest Harbor police reported all was quiet last week. Except for Tuesday, when a Forest Avenue woman phoned police to complain about a neighbor's dog who repeatedly stole cat food off her porch.*

In 1796 Bar Harbor belonged to Massachusetts, and the state government chose to call it Eden in honor of an English statesman. Locals, being more practical, called it Bar Harbor because of the sand bar that connects Mount Desert to Bar Island at low tide. After 125 years the government—now Maine's—finally gave in and officially changed the name to Bar Harbor.

In the 1820s and 1830s Bar Harbor became a playground for yachtsmen who hiked and climbed and hunted in the forest. And it was the artwork of landscape painters Thomas Cole and Frederic Church in the mid-1800s that attracted others to "Eden." The tourists then were known as "rusticators" or "summercators." They were put up at first by local families, but as more came over the years, by train and boat from Boston, Philadelphia,

Washington, Chicago, from all over, hotels grew in number and size until they hit 30 in 1880, including one atop Cadillac Mountain and one (the Rodick House) that was the biggest summer hotel in the country. Clearly Mount Desert was *the* place to be in summer; wealthy families—the Rockefellers, Vanderbilts, Pulitzers, Morgans, Astors—all built lavish cottages. To make sure the island stayed the way they liked it, many of those prominent families contributed to the creation of the National Park. Under the leadership of Charles Eliot and George Bucknam Dorr, the rusticators put together a land trust at the turn of the century and, in 1916, officially established the first National Park east of the Mississippi.

In 1917 John D. Rockefeller, Jr. designed and built the first of the 50 miles of Carriage Paths (intended, literally, for carriages) and 16 hand-cut stone bridges which would become such notable features of the Park. The carriage roads are wide, gently sloped paths with stunning views of Somes Sound (the only fjord on the Atlantic coast) and the Atlantic beyond; of Jordan Pond, Bubble Pond, or Eagle Lake; of Blue Hill Bay; Cadillac Mountain; of frozen creeks, trees, and sky. They pass through poplar and birch, coated in ice on my visit, that grew up after the great fire of 1947 destroyed much of a spruce and fir forest.

Acadia is unique among the other parks in the National Park system, in that the vast majority of it consists of lands donated to the Park. In fact, of the 35,000 acres within the Park, only the first 6,000 acres assembled in 1904, were <u>not</u> donated. Jack Hauptman, the Superintendent of the Park, said they were created "with a perception of what the Park's values are, and designed in a way to take you to them. In a fashion unlike any other National Park, Acadia is a <u>landscaped</u> park."

I drove to the base of Cadillac Mountain on my second morning in town. Cadillac Mountain was named by French explorer Antoine de la Mothe Cadillac who took possession of the island in the late 1600s and later founded Detroit. If Cadillac Mountain were a car, it would be a pink Cadillac, since the granite underfoot is a pink feldspar with glassy quartz, and blackish hornblende.

I skied that morning through some of the park's landscaped forest, from Parkman Mountain to Jordan Pond. At the top, 1,530 feet, I had reached the park's highest spot—the highest spot on the Atlantic Coast north of Brazil. If I had made it there at dawn, I would've been the first in the nation to see the sun's rays. It is also the island's best lookout: To the east islands dot Frenchman Bay, with the Schoodic Peninsula beyond; to the south are the Cranberry Islands, Seal Harbor, and the open sea.

A Bar Harbor sailor once told me that in summer, from his boat out on Frenchman Bay on the north side of the island, he could see cars lined bumper to bumper on the road to the summit of Cadillac Mountain. But now the unplowed road made a perfect path for my ascent on skis. It took me the rest of the morning to reach the top, with frequent stops to view the interior of the island and Eastern Bay, a splendid way to spend a sunny winter's day. In that time I saw only two people, but tracks of deer and fox and snowshoe hare were everywhere, and on the edge of Jordan Pond, I found the cradle of an otter slide. My ski to the bottom passed in one long, continuous schuss. It matched the best backcountry skiing I have ever done.

That night the full moon shone so brightly on the snow-covered Park Loop Road that I drove with my headlights off to Blackwood Campground on the southern tip of the island. Even Blackwood, with every one of its 300 campsites normally in use in summer, was entirely mine; it was as peaceful a night as I can remember. In the morning I crawled out of my tent early enough to snowshoe through the empty campground to a bluff above the ocean and watch the sun rise through a bank of clouds, the clouds parting only when the sun was just above the horizon, so that it perched there on the Atlantic like the Wizard of Oz's head. I was quite sure I had never snowshoed beside an ocean before. I found a dry spot on a piece of driftwood bleached to the color of a peeled almond, leaned back against a spruce, propped my snowshoes up and had my breakfast, and vowed that I'd never come back in summer.

Silent, Light

(2015)

I went to church in a tiny church in a nearly nonexistent town on the winter solstice last year. I could have gone to any number of churches closer to where I live, in the Farmington-Wilton area, but I particularly wanted to see this one, so I drove an hour north and west into the remoteness of Madrid Township, turning off Route 4 onto Reeds Mills Road about 15 miles before Rangeley, and then five miles further to where a few cars were parked beside the road. I looked around: no church, just trees and more trees. Then I got out of the car and saw the narrow snow-covered drive that led to the building a hundred yards away. I joined the quiet clusters of people walking along in the lengthening shadows of 3 p.m. on a day when the sun would set at 4:03.

There were probably many old, small, hidden churches at use on that solstice Sunday in Maine. But I'd heard about this one in the fall, and attending a service there appealed to me, for reasons which may make sense to some people. The Reeds Mill Church, also known as "the Little Church in the Wildwood," has a grace, the kind of grace that comes from modesty in every aspect. The church is old—built in 1892—and a model of perfect proportions; it has the sharpest, cleanest lines to every wall and angle, with four windows on each side, two doors in front, another window centered between the doors and slightly above the tops of the doors; a diamond-shaped window directly above that window and midway between it and the roof peak; a large belfry at the top front. No attached shed or new additions, no orna-mentation, just a perfectly rectangular box; so spare, the bath-room is an outhouse.

The church reminded me of that ancient Greek ideal, of the golden ratio, where the relationship of the length of the shorter side to the longer side (in this case, the front and back) is a fac-tor of 1.618033 and change. I didn't measure it before I stepped inside, but I am convinced the building is proportioned along those lines.

Inside, what heat there was came from a wood stove, and the music wheezed out of a pump organ, the kind where the organ-ist pushes down on foot pedals which operate a bellows which generates the tone. The sheet metal stove in the rear had been burning for hours, and the heat was transported by the longest stove pipe in all of Franklin County. It rose up a few feet from the stove, then began angling towards the ceiling and towards the front of the church, passing over the heads of the congregation settling into the ten pews, then took a left and exited through the ceiling. Beneath the stove pipe, one was cozy; the further away from it one sat, the more coats and hats stayed on. Three candles and greenery had been arranged on the inside of each window, and a half dozen large kerosene lanterns hung from the ceiling, the only illumination in this building without electricity.

The service had that holiday mixture, Christian and ecumen-ical, with prayers and a bit of a sermon from Ginni Robie, a local woman who has taken a leading role in preserving the Reeds Mills church. But mostly it was singing, with attendees calling out song titles for the organist to play. Usually we sang the first verse of the carol, maybe two verses, so that everyone had a chance to have their favorites sung. The organist, Ann, began to slide off the bench after a while because of her foot pumping action, so her husband left his pew to slip around behind her, braced him-self against a wall, and held her in place with his knees. As the service went on and the light dimmed, Ann pulled on a headlamp in order to read the music.

By the end we were all tilting our hymnals towards the windows to read the lyrics, as the day vanished and the lanterns couldn't throw enough light. We could still see well enough to get through "The Little Church in the Wildwood" (#367 in the hymnal), which is sung at every gathering in the Reeds Mills church. The service concluded with "Silent Night" and candles being lit and passed. Then the church emptied for another seven months, until summer services begin in July. The perfectly proportioned church, tucked back in its own half acre off a back road, fell silent as the last of the congregation drifted down the snow-covered drive. A little light remained inside, fading slowly.

Three

Magnetic

These pieces were inspired by the inherent interest of the sub-ject. They are therefore an eclectic group, ranging from a man who adopted a Maine persona and lived in a way appropriate to that identity, to the culture of firewood and wood stoves, to those of us who are taken by hand-colored photographs such as the ones Charles Sawyer produced.

"The Tallest Lady in the World", was the first article I wrote once we'd moved to Wilton, where my wife and I still live. We'd moved up from Connecticut after one year there while my wife had a one-year position at a college. While we waited for the house we'd bought to become available on the first of September, we rented a one-bedroom apartment in a tiny duplex on a side street in Wilton, and the five of us, including the dog, tried to survive close quarters for two months. To escape the confines of the duplex, I sometimes went to the library in town, the Wilton Free Public Library, which was and is the soul of the town.

Working on the syllabus I would use for my first semester of teaching at Colby College, I noticed a display near where I was sitting at one of the long oak tables. It was a mannequin, in a tall display case, in the shape of a very tall woman dressed in an outfit typical of the mid-1800s. High necked, one long stretch of fabric, a dull color. Going closer I read the label on the display, which said something like "Sylvia Hardy, Wilton resident. At one time the tallest lady in the world."

I asked around town and found someone who had started gathering materials for a history of Sylvia, and with that and the help of the Maine State Library and other Wilton residents who knew the story, I pulled together the somewhat sad story of Sylvia Hardy. I liked telling her story, and the fact that the subject caught me—the local woman who was the tallest woman in the world—is exactly is how I've taken up other topics. I become interested for whatever reason, and that's enough to get me going.

These appeared in *Yankee*, *Maine Décor*, and *Down East*, between 1988 and 2020. "The Northwoods Balladeer" was previously unpublished.

The Art of the Myth
(2002)

The auctioneer's helper takes the picture off the wall, and I watch its journey to the table at the front of the hall. But first, though, there is a cat-shaped tea pot to be sold, and a set of plated Sheffield utensils, then a box of old books, including an early edition of *Treasure Island*. Finally the auctioneer holds up what I am there for.

"This here's a Sawyer, folks, pretty little thing," he says turning it over and back. "Doesn't have a title but it's all in good shape—shows a dirt road through a forest." He pauses, waiting for suspense to build. "Who'll give me a hundred dollars to get it started, one hundred dollars, a hundred dollars now . . ." and he slides into his song.

I enter the bidding when it drops to thirty dollars and by fifty dollars it is just me and another man seated a few rows ahead of me. At sixty-five I think I've won, but so does he, and the auctioneer is confused, so we start again, only the two of us allowed to bid. By then my discipline is gone; we go back and forth in small increments until, at ninety dollars, I've won (or lost, as my wife claims later).

An embarrassed grin on my face, I watch the helper come down the aisle with my prize: a tiny, two-and-a-half inch by five-and-a-half inch hand-colored photograph, showing—just as the auctioneer had said—nothing but a dirt road curving through a woods. My wife takes it from me and glances at it, then passes it back. "How much did you pay for that again?" she asks.

The colors of a Sawyer print glow: oranges and reds and yellows, as though fall has been distilled to just these colors. In another, spring is apple trees in bloom dappled white, pink and green in the foreground, in a way that is just slightly more colorful than life, with a row of familiar mountains behind.

Sawyer prints are a passion for some, a puzzle to others. Along with two Portland-based photographers, Charles Bicknell and Fred Thompson, and a host of lesser, regional photographers, Charles Sawyer produced hand-colored photographs for more than a half-century, starting at the end of the 19th. His career lasted longer than most, until the 1950s, although his most valued prints are those from 1900-1930. These are iconic and romanticized New England scenes—rivers and lakes and autumn and birches—and one can purchase them today only at country auctions, yard sales, antique shops, perhaps on eBay. Sawyer prints summon up the revered Maine, but might also raise the question, are they art, or kitsch, photographic pointillism, or pointless?

Sawyer was a native of Norridgewock, that one-stoplight town along Route 2 where Route 201A heads off for Canada, and which is usually famous only for being the site of the massacre of the French Jesuit priest Father Rale and his Abenaki followers, by English forces in 1724. This is where Sawyer was born in 1868, and lived until the late 1800s. If you're a fan of Sawyer you can stand in the parking lot at the junction of Route 2 and 139 and gaze reverentially at the Cumberland Farms store, the spot on which the family business, the Sawyer Hotel, stood until the late 1800s, and where Charles was raised.

Norridgewock is on the banks of the Kennebec River. The

river comes south and east from Anson, and after Norridgewock loops to the east and north to Skowhegan. In town, facing north, you can see the Bigelow Range; you see, in fact, the beginning of the North Woods. The roads out of town dip beside creeks or through woods, or lift you into open fields beyond which are a border of trees, then a row of mountains. It doesn't take long with Sawyer prints to realize where his subjects came from: he was born among them.

One of the early practioners of the (art? craft? process?) trade was Wallace Nutting, a retired minister in Providence, Rhode Island. Nutting dominated the hand-coloring scene, and made it a national enterprise. He was a leading figure in the Arts and Crafts revival, and respect for his furniture as well as his photography has increased dramatically lately. He also influenced all of the "second-tier" of hand-colorists, which, according to Michael Ivankovich, an expert on Nuttings and "Nutting-like" photography, included Sawyer, Thompson, and David Davidson of Providence. Nutting established the methods, too.

The photographer chose the scenes, took the photo and developed it, then turned it over to his colorists, if he didn't color it himself. At first the colorists added water colors, according to the directions of the photographer, or perhaps by reading from a list of instructions prepared by the head colorist. The early prints were all made on platinum-based paper, which took water colors well; later, the platinum paper was replaced by silver-based or a bromide paper. The latter was a good base for oils, so one can guess the relative age of a hand-colored photograph by seeing whether it is a water color or oil.

Sawyer, who was taking photographs as early as the late 1800's, apprenticed to Nutting about 1902-03 in Providence. In 1900 he had moved 15 miles west of Norridgewock to Farmington with his wife Mary and son Harold. He opened his business, the Sawyer Picture Studio, in 1904, in the Drummond Hall on Broadway in Farmington (another reverential moment can be had by standing in front of the current Farmington House of Pizza, where Drummond Hall stood until 1972). To connoisseurs, it is this period, until he left for Concord, New Hampshire. in 1920, that is the golden age of Sawyer prints, and the best of his work—to his admirers at least—is that set in west-central Maine: Norridgewock to Wilton, north to Eustis. We might extend the Golden Age to 1930, but after 1930 a certain modernity and desperation for national exposure creeps in, both in techniques and settings. The era of mass-produced lithographs and lacquered prints began (no serious collector covets them), as did the choice of non-Maine, and even non-New England settings. He took photos of New Hampshire places, such as Echo Lake and the Old Man of the Mountains (shockingly pedestrian), and on several western trips tried out Yosemite and Pacific scenes, but these simply will not do—there is hardly a clearer example to be found of the difference an empathy for a place makes in the artistic rendering of it, than in seeing a Sawyer Yosemite and a Sawyer "Mt. Blue, Valley View," side by side. But Sawyer could do rural Maine, lovingly, which were the prints that came out of the Farmington studio. Carol Begley Gray, Sawyer's only biographer, confirms the superiority of the Farmington-era work, writing that, "The earlier prints from the Farmington studio should demand a somewhat higher price . . ."

Nellie Farmer, a Farmington native, had been Sawyer's chief colorist in his Maine years. When he moved to Concord, Nellie went with him to train the colorists, chief among whom was Gladys Towle. Gladys was a teenager then, yet became the head colorist, and worked for the Sawyer company for 53 years, and instructed the others (all women) who were hired on a piece-work basis to color the photos. The business was at its peak in 1925 and gradually declined during the Depression years and immediately thereafter, but picked up again for a time in the 30's and 40's. By then Sawyer and other hand-colored photographs were "widely accepted as a means of decoration," according to Earl

Shuttleworth, Director of the Maine Historic Preservation Commission, and an expert on early photography in Maine. "They were purchased as souvenirs of travel, too."

Charles died in 1954 and his son, Harold, took over and ran the company for another 18 years, until Gladys Towle retired in 1972. Production of prints fell off then, though the company kept going until 1980. The studio closed in that year, on Harold's death. By the end, there were 2,500 negatives in the Sawyer archive, most of them heavy glass plates.

I thought that must have been the end of the Sawyer picture business, having outlasted Nutting or any other hand-coloring enterprise, until I went into Trask's Jewelers in downtown Farmington. When I asked the sales lady about some modern Sawyers they had for sale, I learned that a man named Harold Yeaton in Concord was still running a Sawyer picture business, and in fact a customer could place an order in Trask's for an image of one's choice, and eventually (production is <u>very</u> limited) would receive a hand-colored photograph made from the original Sawyer negative, albeit a lacquered one.

And the era of hand-colored photographs <u>still</u> continues in Maine. I talked to one such artist recently, Donna Lee Rollins, owner of Silver Image Resources in Portland, who teaches classes in the (art? craft? here we go again), and produces her own hand-colored photos. "I like being able to manipulate the image in a tangible way," she said. "And I like the durability of oils, compared to the fugitive quality of the dyes used in color photography today."

The archaeological study of Sawyer prints involves subjects, matting, frames, signatures, titles, labels. For instance, the distinctive penciled Sawyer signature (the "y" in Sawyer dropping low and with a u-shaped tail, and a straight horizontal line cutting through both sides of the tail) was probably drawn by just one woman, Etabelle Evans, who specialized in signatures; in more modern Sawyers the signature may be a white ink mark stamped on the picture itself. The matting can suggest time and place as well, with images that have a depressed mat into which the picture is set, representing the Farmington period, and perhaps a little after. As noted, Maine scenes often come from the Farmington years, and a grey mat to which the photo was affixed also indicates Farmington.

There are a variety of reasons to collect Sawyers. One is that they are, in fact, collectibles now: Images that sold for $2 in 1924, and for $15-20 five years ago, now sell for $100 to $200 at an auction or in an antique store. The local angle is another appeal, and many owners gravitate towards images of places familiar to them. A former administrator at the University of Maine at Farmington, Tony McLaughlin, has about two dozen Sawyers, most of them of the Farmington and Wilton areas, including one of the most lovely Sawyers, called "Among the New England Hills," set on Voter Hill above Farmington.

The hand-coloring means that each of the early ones is by definition unique. This was reinforced for me when I visited the Norridgewock Historical Society recently. Several local women had brought in their prints for me to see, and two of them happened to be the same picture, "Sunset on the Kennebec." This is a well-known image, showing a road beside the Kennebec River between Skowhegan and Norridgewock, looking upstream towards Norridgewock. When I held the pictures side by side I could see the coloring was entirely different: the shadows across the road were different, the texture of the road itself was, too, and most noticeable of all, the clouds in one had been given a rosy, sunset glow; in the other the clouds were muted and dark, as though sunset were over. It was a reminder that each print was rare, because they had been manipulated by someone, perhaps Gladys Towle, or Nellie Farmer.

Another sign of the individuality of a Sawyer print was the

appearance in Norridgewock of a black and white Sawyer ("black and white prints are not very common and are very collectible," writes Carol Begley Gray) which I immediately recognized, since I own the same one. But mine is titled, "Wilson Stream" (Wilson Stream being the stream that runs through Wilton, our town), while this one was called " 'Neath Towering Elms." None of us in the Historical Society building could come up with an explanation for the difference.

Perhaps a part of Sawyer's charm, too, is that the stable subject—the photo—is overlaid by a unique scrim of color which transforms the scene in a distinct way and makes each a "made" art object. As Earl Shuttleworth said, "Sawyers and other hand-colored photography ask the question of where the photography leaves off and the art begins." Indeed, spend enough time among them and one can feel the subtle tension in a Sawyer, a tension between the photograph and the paint.

The appeal of Sawyer prints is complex, unless, like my wife, you are immune to it. I've often thought that the sign which greets drivers coming over the Piscataqua Bridge should read, "Maine: The Way Life <u>Used</u> To Be" because so many of us are invested in a vision of the state as a place that perpetuates a glorious past. Sawyer pictures speak to that condition. They confirm a beautiful, bucolic history for us, and they enlarge familiar places, deifying and mythifying them. This mythification of our landscape is why so many of the most successful Sawyer scenes are ones that celebrate rather ordinary views, more so than those that record the overly familiar (Echo Lake and Yosemite).

Ultimately, the appeal of a Sawyer is personal, and one is likely to be motivated more by the nostalgia for the scene, or the memories it evokes, than by artistic concerns. Richard Rydel, owner of Brindl Fine Arts Center in St. George, and an expert on 19th and 20th century photography and folk arts, says of Sawyers, "They don't really flip the switch for the professional photography community, not like the really exquisite hand-coloring done by Japanese artists even earlier. There's a real division here: Hand-colored photographs aren't taken seriously within the photographic community, but are attractive to those outside that community. I don't know why."

Back at the auction house, I pay for my purchase and am preparing to leave. A friend who has been at the auction appears at my side and kids me about my triumph. We banter about it, about the divide between those, like me, who will pay $90 for an obscure Sawyer, and those, like him, who don't get it. As my wife and I head out of the building, a tall, older man steps forward.

"That's a rare one," he says, pointing at the Sawyer.

I look doubtfully at him. "It doesn't have a label, it doesn't have a title, it's tiny . . ."

"Those miniatures are valuable," he says, "there aren't many of them around." He takes it from me and looks at it fondly, then passes it back.

Laughing, I offer it to him, as though desperate to get rid of it. "Well, I'll sell it to you."

He doesn't hesitate. "I'll give you more than you paid for it."

My wife and I are shocked into silence. Finally my wife wonders, "Do you know how much he paid?"

The man nods. He says again, "I'll give you more than you paid."

I look at the Sawyer, balancing the ninety dollars and it, weighing the "art" versus "kitsch" debate. Besides, I've got other Sawyers; I don't need this one, and I can restore the $90 to my wallet, restore my wife's faith in my economic prudence.

I mounted it just below another Sawyer, "Mt. Blue, Valley View" on my den wall.

The Northwoods Balladeer
(2007)

No one would ever come upon Burdin Corner, Maine, by accident. To get there you must pass through places with grand names like Athens, Harmony, Wellington, and Dog Corner; drive on roads which seem to disappear from beneath you as you travel on them; then, when you have given up any hope of arriving, come to the top of a ridge, with a view to the north of a thousand other ridges, and find nothing but a church and a steeple at the place where two dirt roads cross. Burdin Corner.

On an August Sunday a surprisingly large congregation has gathered. The crowd, four hundred or so, is here for the "Hill Country Hoedown," a fundraiser for the restoration of the tiny church. Bluegrass bands, fiddlers and folk singers take turns performing, and the field behind the chapel is filled with pickups and trailers. There are a few mean-looking Harleys around, a man with a life-size tattoo of a Bowie knife on his upper arm, and one canvas tent.

Sitting in front of the tent, in an ancient felt hat with a toothbrush stuck into the band of the brim, is the man I am after, Matthew Heintz, *aka* "The Northwoods Balladeer."

When I find him, the Balladeer is bagging up beef jerky, which he has just finished smoking in the tent. He swaps the jerky with the small knot of people who are gathered around, all of whom seem to be waiting expectantly, whether for his jerky or for one of his tales, I can't tell. Matthew has a story for almost anything he comes across, and he passes these out along with the jerky.

Matthew is a man of several talents, all of them, well, odd, and I have come to see him precisely because of this profligacy. He has been many things in his life so far, including pig farmer, deckhand, and canoe-maker, but right now he is three specifically odd things: a beef jerky epicure; a dump scavenger; and the Balladeer.

These skills are not mere dabblings, but essential ingredients of the life Matthew has fashioned for himself. Although the nature of his appeal is hard to define, one can say that, at the least, Matthew is a rare bird.

Matthew is 43 years old, of average height, and is somehow both sturdy-looking and gnomish at the same time. He has a round face that is nearly lost in the black swamp of his beard, and his laugh is one of those hearty bursts that only country people seem to have.

He was born in Maine, but left when he was just two, for Ohio, where his father was the head librarian at Oberlin College. Rejecting the scholarly life ("Our house was wall to wall books," he says, in his hard-to-place mix of Midwest and Maine accents. "I felt as though I was suffocating in them"), he bounced out of Ohio State after a short time and ended up in Seattle, where he found a job as a deckhand on a U.S. research ship that went on a six-month tour of the South Pacific.

Having discovered the vagabond's life, he drifted, landed, and moved on; from Seattle to Santa Fe, to Ohio, with stints as a maker of leather clothes, a truck driver, caretaker, bartender, scenery-maker for theatre, and as a sometime songwriter.

In 1988 he came home to Maine. Even then he wanderered, from Weld to Wiscasset and then out to Wolfe's Neck Farm near Freeport. In the winter of 1990 he was drawn upstate to the Dover-Foxcroft area by an acquaintance with a like-minded spirit, a yurt-maker from the region. He spent the rest of the winter in an un-insulated camp in nearby Atkinson where he hunkered down, riding out the cold. In the spring, when he walked once more in the woods, he noticed patches of blue metal in the underbrush. Rooting around he discovered what they were: graniteware pots, marking the site of a farm's abandoned dump. Intrigued by the idea of digging through rubble to unearth treasures, he began performing this dump archaeology, and selling his finds at flea markets on the coast.

That spring he also started working at the Island Falls canoe company in Atkinson. It was while he was laboring alongside the owner, famed canoe-maker Jerry Stelmok, on traditional-design, wood and canvas canoes, that Matthew began to pass time by telling stories, his not-quite-fiction, not-quite-true tales of his life and the North Woods. Then he began singing them as ditties, making up silly songs, like a father might for his child.

Finally, perhaps out of frustration, Stelmok said, "Matthew, you've got to tell someone else these stories!" It was even Stelmok who suggested the name, "The Northwoods Balladeer." On a Sunday in August of 1990, Matthew played in public for the first time, at this very same Burdin Corner Hoedown.

Since then he has performed at dozens of places in Maine, including cafes in Portland and Blue Hill, and at festivals, hoe-downs, fly-ins, and fairs. He dresses for the part, sometime in buckskins, most often in heavy wool pants, LL Bean hunting boots, chamois shirt and the ubiquitous felt hat. And the weird thing is, it works: people love the Northwoods Balladeer.

Back at the Hoedown, Matthew is a busy man. It seems nearly every cluster of people has one of Matthew's bags of jerky, and the sight of jaws working furiously on the tough, sweet chew is a ubiquitous one.

Matthew's jerky, the result of two decades of experimentation, is what a connoisseur might call "an exotic yet rugged" taste. It is sweet, tart, and tough, all at the same time. Making it requires the right recipe (a secret, naturally, although red wine and Worcestshire sauce are involved), the right tent (canvas), the right method (four hours of slicing, 48 for marinating, and 12 to 20 for smoking), and the right fuel: green apple wood. "I've tried everything," Matthew says, "but nothing else burns so sweet."

Later, Matthew gives me a bag of the jerky, which I plan on taking home and sharing with the family. As I start out on the hundred-mile drive home I sample a bite of the stout strip and somehow the rest disappears between Burdin Corner and home.

A week after the Hoedown I went with Matthew on one of his farm dump digs. We stopped at the kitchen door of a sagging farmhouse in Atkinson and asked permission from the elderly woman whose home since childhood this had been. After receiving a blessing on our digging, we headed off.

Farm dump digging, while it has been a money-maker for Matthew in the past, is now mostly an amusement. He finds the dumps in the fall, when he goes partridge hunting in the late evening or early morning. The best way to hunt partridge, he says, is by walking the stone walls on the old farms, and sometimes, if the light is right and he isn't distracted by an actual partridge, he will see the rusty metal wheel from a farm tool, or a glint of glass, and he will know he's on to something. But if he sees plastic, he passes on. As he says, with a sniff, "Why would I want to dig through someone's garbage?" Plastic is a sign of modernity, and Matthew wants only the pre-WWII dumps, with their more interesting loot.

"There are some rules for dump-picking," he announced as we walked. "One is that no one ever threw the trash uphill, so always look for the downhill part of a farm. And no one ever took trash very far, so look at the end of a clearing."

And that was where we found it at this homestead, just beyond a crumbling stone wall at one end of a field. The dump was simply a pile of metal and bottles—and, let's face it, junk—that meant absolutely nothing to me, until Matthew began digging and talking. Certain things float to the top of a dump, said Matthew; graniteware for instance, and old barrel hoops. Bottles, on the other hand, tend to sink, and bottles are often the most valuable part of a dump.

Using a long-handled rake, we pulled up the parts to a coal parlor stove, including a plate which had the single word "Home" on it, a touching reminder of the connection between hearth and home. Matthew held up an innocuous-looking bottle and beamed, and when I looked unimpressed, announced that this was an amethyst bottle, made from glass that has manganese in it, which, when left in the sunlight for long enough, takes on a purplish hue. The bottle might be worth only a little, but it was pleasing to the eye in any case.

We also found the porcelain liners to the zinc lids of fruit jars, a worthless item until several years ago when Matthew began selling them to artists. Matthew's tastes in digging are eclectic, but he has an eye for potential, and knows that old whiskey, poison, or bitters bottles can bring as much as $700.

As we picked I found myself getting caught up by it, by the thrill of discovery, of now knowing what is below the weeds, leaves, roots, and other debris, and the knowledge that it could be—might be, probably isn't—something valuable. I found an old apothecary's bottle, which was utterly worthless, Matthew informed me, but it had such odd and interesting figures on it that I kept it anyway.

After the dig, we retired to Matthew's home for a beer. Matthew lives now in a one-room camp outside of Atkinson (Atkinson is just slightly more cosmopolitan than Burdin Corner).

An improvement on his first Atkinson residence, this camp has electricity and insulation, but no running water. The camp is filled with artifacts of Matthew's lives, mostly from his career in dump-picking. There is a cast-iron penny bank that he found in a farm dump not far away, worth $150 or so (a story goes with the bank, naturally, too long to recount here; with Matthew, there is always a story), and a string of bottle necks hang in the window, prisms throwing a rainbow of color when the sun pours through them. The canvas jerky tent is bundled up and stored outside, and out back sits Dan Neal's birch-bark canoe, whose story is worth telling.

Dan Neal was a legendary Maine guide and canoe maker around the turn of the 19th century. After Matthew arrived in Atkinson and heard of Dan Neal, he decided to write a song about him, called "The Ballad of Buttermilk Pond," which has become one of his more popular creations. It is a funny, goofy ditty, which evokes that mythic-Maine, the Golden Age of the 20s or so, that many of us want to believe we still live in. It includes such lines as "You see, Dan had this bark canoe he treated like a pet/He even gave it a name/He fed it cedar chips daily and taught it to fetch/cause he knew that canoe of his was destined for fame." Matthew called the canoe, Clem.

After Matthew performed the song a few times, he received a letter from a man in North Carolina who said that he in fact owned that canoe. The idea that a canoe he had invented from whole cloth turned out to be made of birch bark, was startling to Matthew, so he wrote back, and eventually bought the canoe. When Matthew had the canoe in hand he noticed that a few ribs had been broken and repaired, and no doubt he felt a Twilight Zone-ish tingle: for his song, written before he knew that the canoe existed, included these lines: "So Clem the canoe paddled hard through the ice/bucking a strong head wind all of the time/he poked a hole through his bark/and broke three ribs twice." Matthew may be a backwoods psychic, his canoe and his song connecting to each other across time, space, and several dimensions.

In a fashion this is the goal of his balladeering: "I guess what I'm doing in the songs is trying to recreate the atmosphere of the turn-of-the-century hunting or logging camp in Maine," Matthew told me that evening as we watched the sun set over one of the ridges outside Atkinson. "The old woods camps always had one guy who was basically a singer, whatever other job he had in the camp, and at night he would sing for the men. I want to keep the tradition of those singers alive."

Matthew's turn to perform at the Hoedown has come and there is an expectant hush as he sets up. In a small way it is like the return of the star to the stage where he got his start, the Beatles returning to The Cavern Club in Liverpool. Matthew sings his songs, about canoes, and pig-farming, and being lonely, and moose, and the audience laughs and sings along when he asks them to. It is a gentle performance, acoustic, simple, and only slightly ironic, and it is so very Maine.

This may be the secret of Matthew's appeal: everything he does reminds us of Maine, but not the one we actually live in. It is that other Maine that he honors, the vanished one, of woods camps, birch bark canoes, jerky tents, Maine Guides, sporting camps, and moose. As with Dan Neal's canoe, he connects us to that Maine despite the difficult barriers of time and space.

Burning

(2015)

A hot and muggy day in July, one of those days when to move is to sweat. I have sweated through my t-shirt, my pants, through my hat, through my boots even, and I am covered in wood chips. It is like being in Vulcan's forge, laboring away on behalf of the god of fire. In July, firewood seems useless.

I am sawing up trees that have been cut from our land. We don't have a wood lot *per se*, but our trees need thinning from time to time, and the thinning has left about a cord-and-a-half of our own trees to deal with. I am turning the four-foot long hunks of tree into 16-inch pieces that will fit our stove. As I work, as I sweat, I am reminded of that old line we repeat to each other when we complain about heating with wood: "It warms you four times: when you cut it, when you split it, when you stack it, and when you burn it." (Henry David Thoreau, ever the minimalist, claimed only two warmings: when you cut it and again when you burn it.)

Heating your home with wood is an odd thing, a last vestige of the prehistoric in our lives. Think of it: we willingly make fires in our houses, invite fires inside, share our homes with them. This might someday seem as strange as indoor bathrooms did to the Elizabethans: why would you want all <u>that</u> inside your house?

But fires and their chambers—wood stoves, pellet stoves, fireplace inserts—have a firm grip on us in Maine, where we have two of the best motivations there are for heating with wood: January, and a land mass that is 82% trees.

Of course, not everyone heats with wood, despite our ready supply of it. For those who do, there are three reasons and only three reasons to still dabble in the prehistoric: One is economic, because the BTUs from firewood are much cheaper than those from oil. A cord of hardwood is the equivalent of about 165 gallons of heating oil; I recently paid $3.20 a gallon for oil and $225 for a cord of wood, or $528 against $225 (but you don't have to stack oil). Another is environmental, since wood is a thoroughly renewable and available resource in Maine, and they aren't making any more oil. And the third is aesthetic, the particular and peculiar pleasures of a wood fire.

Oddly, I've never met anyone who is motivated by only one of these reasons, rather than all three, although my neighbor, Norm Gould, a practical native-Mainer and long-time Selectman in Wilton, adds a rare fourth: "Nostalgia value. I grew up with wood fires," he says, including the one he regularly sets in the cook stove, which dates back to 1926, "and I remember that there's nothing like cozying up to a wood fire when it's 15 below outside."

Despite the many virtues of heating with wood, it is not an un-conflicted activity. After all, wood fires do emit particulate, even toxic, matter into the atmosphere. The CO2 released by burning wood is actually greater per BTU than it is for burning the equivalent BTUs of oil. Many cities restrict wood stove burning at certain times of year because of the heavy smoke that can build up, and fires are a constant concern, with about 500 chimney fires started each year in Maine. And let's face it, burning with wood is a lot of work, much more than flicking on the thermostat to get the oil or gas furnace chugging.

But as one friend reminds me, even though burning wood does add CO2, "a woodlot puts away a lot more than we burn." And no one ever warms her hands over a baseboard heat panel or stares transfixed into a hot air register, or comes home and hovers near the thermostat on a frosty day, as you do with a wood stove.

It is easy to find impassioned arguments for the environmental value of heating with wood, but putting all of them aside, one thing must be true for heating with wood to be a net virtue rather than a net problem: population density. Luckily, then, that Maine is a low-density state, 38th in the nation. Which means that in most of the state we can burn wood without breathing each other's smoke.

Heating one's home with wood is a big cycle, a big romantic cycle to some people, even those who have traveled around the cycle for a long time. It is a cycle in the temporal sense, as well as the ecologic: it is a nearly year-round activity, with little time off from cutting, splitting, stacking, burning, cleaning.

Most of my fellow pyrophiles step into the domestic heating cycle as close to the "burning" part as possible, by having their wood delivered—as the phrase goes—"cut and split," meaning they've managed to skip those first two steps in the cycle. Most of us order by the cord, deluding ourselves into thinking that what is delivered is actually the 128 cubic feet a cord is supposed to be. I've measured stacked cords several times, and they are rarely even close. There are a million different explanations for how this can be, but I've learned to accept "cord" as a charming myth.

Very few of us are engaged with the whole cycle, from wood lot to ash can. My old friend, Bob Kimber, a writer, is one of those few. Bob, of Temple, has about 30 acres in his wood lot, and for the last 40 years, all of his firewood has come out of that lot. At 78, he cuts and splits about five cords per year (since it is his own wood, and since it is Bob, the cord is probably exactly 128 cubic feet). He cuts the wood for the following year in fall or early winter, preferably when the ground is frozen, and splits it by axe in place ("I've been known to split pieces as small round as my thumb," he says with a rueful laugh), then hauls it across the road using his old tractor and stores it in a drying shed beside the house, where it is protected from rain and snow, but open to wind.

He has two stoves (<u>everyone</u> has two stoves, it seems): One is a ThermoControl hot water furnace in the kitchen that supplies baseboard heat; another is a Jotul parlor stove in a, well, front parlor. Bob and his wife, Rita, embrace the economic, environmental, and aesthetic about as completely as one could do: they don't have to pay for firewood since they have their own wood lot, so their heat is even cheaper than for the rest of us; they have reduced their carbon footprint by using wood instead of oil, and with the addition of solar panels, they have reduced the oil consumption even further, but not, Bob notes, the amount of wood he burns; and the warmth from wood is, as Bob says, "just heaven."

Terrell Crouch, a retired University of Maine English professor, starts slightly farther along the cycle from the Kimbers. He has his own 50 acres, which he used to harvest himself, but now he hires, or swaps wood with, "a guy with a skidder" who hauls out five or six cords of logs, which Terry then cuts up and splits with a gas-powered splitter. He has two stoves, naturally, one a Stanley Waterford cookstove, which is big enough to hold a fire overnight, and to which he rigged a copper coil for heating hot water; and a Jotul for when it gets really cold. His house is small, he says, and well-insulated, so the five or six cords is all he needs for heat. He heats with wood for all of the usual reasons, including "just the magic of fire, the basic primitiveness of it."

Gretchen Legler, a professor at the University of Maine at Farmington and also a writer, steps into the wood-heating river downstream from both Bob and Terry, when the trees cut from her property have already been felled and "bucked up" (that's wood cutter lingo for cutting trees into the appropriate lengths), but then she and her partner Ruth split it themselves. I asked Gretchen one day what she likes about heating with wood. She paused for just a second, then said, with a writer's dramatic flair, "because it's alive."

I begin my wood season at the stacking phase, right after the "cut-and-split." The arrival of that first load signals the end of the longest unbroken period of not dealing with wood stoves and fires, all the way from mid-May to early July. All those who heat with wood eventually have to stack it, because wood stacking as a profession has not yet been invented. There are many ways to stack firewood, but all of them are wrong, according to at least one other stacker.

If Bob can't get his wood into his drying shed, he stacks it in single-row piles on pallets around his yard; Gretchen and Ruth stack theirs by first making a large circle of slabs on the ground, then tossing pieces onto the circle until it makes a round mound. Another strategy I've seen employed is called by some the "New Brunswick." Here, the wood in a pile is stacked on end, leaning upwards towards a center point. A stack like this ends up looking like a pile of shingles, or like a hairy character from a Roald Dahl book. And there are people who make sculptures out of their stacks, or embed images into them, and the Scandinavians, who make what look like tubs of wood, horizontal pieces radiating out from a center.

My stacks are dull: I stack some of the year's wood inside an attached barn, which requires no special skill; but I also stack a row against the south wall of our barn, about 20 feet long and just under a window, supported by two end-pillars I make by putting two half round pieces in one direction, and on top of those two more set perpendicular to the first, and then back again. Bob Kimber calls it a log cabin or cribworks effect. Even after all these years, I still do it poorly, and sometimes the whole thing crumbles, like defeat in a game of Jenga. If it doesn't collapse, I cover it in clear plastic, and the stack is nicely dry and light when March or April comes and it's time to toss the wood through the barn window.

The point of this exercise in cutting, splitting, and stacking, of course, is to actually burn the wood, to heat the house. Like wood stacking, the choice of how to do the burning can be contentious and personal, and fraught with implications of propriety, dignity, snobbish-ness. While choosing a wood stove is not as complicated, say, as choosing a cell phone, people do have strong feelings about their stoves; I know people who have spent far more on their stoves than on their cars.

The choice now is mostly between pellet stoves and regular wood stoves (and less so the other wood burning devices that are strictly for heat, such as the backyard furnaces that were popular for awhile, then fell into disfavor because of the amount of smoke they blew into neighbor's noses). There are also basement systems, combinations of wood and oil, which burn four-foot logs slowly, then switch to oil heat when the wood burns out.

Marty Farnum, co-owner of Northern Lights Hearth and Sports in Farmington, says the number of stoves they sell has stayed steady over the last ten years, but that he's noticed an evolution in the choices. "After about 30 years, people start moving to pellet stoves, and then to gas stoves," he says. The reason is obvious: stacking. Marty says the switch isn't to save money (it doesn't), or environmental (pellet stoves have about the same CO2 output as regular wood stoves), but just to avoid the labor. "After 30 years, a lot of people just don't want to do it, or can't," he says. Pellet stoves are relatively recent additions to the Maine stove lineup, even though "out west they've been using them for years. They took a long time to catch on here because we've got so many trees. Around here we heat so much more with wood than they do in southern New England. It's tough to beat wood, when you're surrounded by trees. Besides, there's no other way to get that bone-penetrating heat."

In our house, we've had at least five stoves in our 26 years in Maine. When we bought the house in 1987, it came with a huge, heavy Vermont Castings Defiant, plus an old Ashley, with its replaceable sheet metal liner. We added a small parlor stove-knock off, then ruined the Defiant (long story, involving an ice dam in the chimney, South Africa, tire chains, a kerosene blaster, and the help of an old friend), replaced it with a Jotul 3, and added a Regency insert in a den fireplace whose bricks and chimney were too rotten to be used anymore.

Like everything with old houses, you can spend a lot of money to reduce your energy costs, ease your environmental conscience, and improve the aesthetics. We hired a mason to rebuild the chimney from the floor of the attic to above the roof line, got our local stove shop to run a stainless-steel liner down and around some bends in the old flue as it entered the fireplace, and attached it to the insert they installed. After all this we have a solid, safe chimney and a lovely fireplace.

Which we use on Christmas morning.

Well, and a few other especially cold days. Maybe six times a year in all. But it looks great.

At the risk of drawing outrageous conclusions from little evidence, it seems obvious that heating with wood is also a kind of personal statement—it says something about what kind of person you are or want to be, about your values; that you're willing to work for the pleasures of that bone-penetrating heat, that heaven, that you're not afraid to bend and straighten a million times while you cut and stack, that you enjoy the handling of wood and want to keep it a part of your life. At least, this is what I tell myself on those July days, awash in sweat.

So we might have to add another motivation to that list: the tactile. We touch a lot of wood when we heat with it, no matter where we start our cycle, and that touching connects us back to our beginnings. You handle the wood, you feel the fire, you see the flame, you can even smell it; you can even hear it if you've got the stove doors open and a screen in front. Gretchen's comment, "It's alive," rings true then.

There are times when I resent the endless tending, the weekly removal of ashes, the hassles with splitting and stacking, the relentlessly upward price (still cheaper than oil), but sometimes I'll pull out a slab from the wood box and admire it a little—the grain, the color, the sharp smell if it's the right kind of wood, even the clean, smooth lines of a good split—before setting it on the fire, like an offering.

The Tallest Lady In The World (1988)

In 1888 a woman named Sylvia Hardy died. The world took little notice of the event, and both the fact of her passing and the character of her life have almost vanished from record. But Sylvia had been famous once: she was the "Maine Giantess," touted by P.T. Barnum as "The Tallest Lady in the World." At age 46 she was 7′10 ½″ tall, and at her death she weighed about 400 pounds. She may have been the tallest woman in the world during her lifetime, and she was easily the tallest woman ever to have been born in the United States up to that time.

Sylvia was indeed a giant; yet she was also a person, a woman, daughter, friend. How hard it must have been for people of her time (and even our own) to see beyond her giant shadow. It might have been just as difficult for Sylvia herself.

In the last century three women have taken an interest in Sylvia's story and tried to preserve it. The first was Lena Adams, whose husband Harry was a grandnephew of Sylvia's. Much of the family memorabilia was passed down to her, and she in turn passed it to Blanche Applebee, a schoolteacher and writer from North Jay, Maine. In the 1940s and 1950s Applebee gathered what stories she could from the few persons still alive who had known or seen Sylvia and from contemporary news accounts. Before her death in 1985, she turned her materials over to Maxine Scott of Wilton, who is now the unofficial historian of Sylvia

Hardy. If not for the efforts of these three, Sylvia's story might have vanished forever.

Sylvia was born on August 17, 1823, in Wilton, a little town on the shore of Wilson Pond, midway between Rangeley and Lewiston, north and south, and Farmington and Rumford, east and west. Her father was John Hardy, son of William, one of the early settlers in town, and her mother was Jane Dalley. Sylvia was the first child of the Hardys, and she weighed but five pounds at birth. Apparently she had a twin brother who died at four months, and according to the wisdom of the day, this accounted for Sylvia's eventual size, she having "taken" the growth from her twin. Sylvia's father died when she was seven, and her mother married Benjamin Leonard and was widowed by him, too.

Sylvia's early childhood was essentially a normal, unremarkable one. Giants are not born, of course, nor are they created in one spectacular burst; they result from growing at an abnormally rapid rate, a process that may continue into their thirties. Sylvia started her schooling when not quite three years old and didn't take any noticeable size until she was 12. She went through a stage of tremendous growth then, and at 18, weakened by the unnaturally swift changes, she broke a hip and was always slightly lame thereafter. A picture of her taken about this time shows an attractive, stylish young woman, rather sober-faced, with a set, down-turned mouth, and a thin scarf wound and knotted around her head.

As a young woman Sylvia worked "out," which in those days meant lodging temporarily with a family to assist during an illness or after the birth of a child. She was an uncommonly good nurse, by all accounts, in particular because she could hold a baby entirely in one hand, the baby's head resting on her fingertips, its legs on her wrist, while she did housework with the other hand.

Her life seems to have proceeded in this fashion through her twenties and thirties: still growing, working in neighbors' houses, living with her widowed mother. She might have remained a local oddity if it hadn't been for a fellow named Leon Bump, who lived in Wilton at the time. Leon had a cousin from Middleboro, Massachusetts—Lavinia Bump—who was a midget, standing 31 inches tall. In 1863 Lavinia married the famous "General Tom Thumb," Charles S. Stratton, also a midget, who was star of P.T. Barnum's American Museum in New York City. Lavinia use to visit Leon in Wilton, and it was inevitable that the tiny lady should be introduced to the giant one. So it was in the spring of 1871 Sylvia was persuaded to leave her home and her mother and join Barnum's New York show as "The Tallest Lady in the World."

Like many other questions about her, the question of Sylvia's actual size is now impossible to answer. Barnum, or course, exaggerated it, just as he introduced Charles Stratton to the world as General Tom Thumb, declaring that he was 11 years old and an Englishman, when in fact he was only six and from Connecticut. George Goding, who as a boy in 1880 boarded with Sylvia and her mother while he attended school in Wilton, claimed that Barnum had Sylvia wear built-up shoes and striped dresses in order to make her look even taller. Still, the height of 7′10 ½″ seems to have been accepted by many witnesses. The Portland *Argus* reported that at age 30, Sylvia had been 7′6″, weighed 300 pounds, and was still growing.

In addition, one of the few surviving photographs of Sylvia, taken while she was with Barnum, wearing a silk dress now owned by the Wilton Historical Society, distinctly shows that she suffered from acromegaly, a progressive enlargement of the hands, feet, nose, lips, tongue, and lower jaw, which, while not the result of giantism, is caused by an irregular pituitary gland, as is giantism. Her dress in Wilton measures 6′8″; add ten or 12 inches to account for her head and neck, and take away a few to allow for Barnum's platform shoes, and it seems safe to say that she was well over seven feet tall.

She was on exhibit for ten weeks in New York, then went with Barnum when he turned his museum into a traveling circus, on tour in New England and the West. The show traveled in large coaches over rough, rutted country roads. On these journeys General and Mrs. Thumb would get tossed about so badly that Sylvia would take one in each hand and support them until the worst parts were over.

At the end of her brief career with Barnum, Sylvia traveled for a time with a Colonel Wood, who had a show that toured the U.S. and Cuba; then, she returned to Wilton to the house on Depot Street she had bought for her mother and herself. There she began another chapter in her life. When she joined Barnum's show, she had developed an interest in the "science" of Spiritualism. She decided that she was a medium and that it was her task to convert all the world to Spiritualism.

She held séances in her house nearly every night for the last 15 or so years of her life. These were open to anyone she could get to come, although most of those who attended seem to have been local young men. Participants remembered that she would all but drag people off the streets in order to have enough gathered around the table for the séance. One person recalled how spooky these sessions were, with a giant invoking the spirits who would respond by means of thunderous raps on the table. Apparently it was a regular occurrence for the table to lift itself off the ground, drawn to Sylvia's hands, which she held a few inches above its top. Harry Adams, her grandnephew, recalled one famous incident in which several men took hold of the legs of the table and tried to prevent it from moving around the room. In one version of the story the legs of the table actually came off without inhibiting its wild dance. "There was something about the way that table seemed to fight back—exactly as if you was wrestling with something alive," said Harry. Adding to the strangeness of the scene was the report that Sylvia's hairpins would pop out of her hair during the séance.

Otherwise, she seemed to live a quiet life in Wilton and mostly a healthy one until the arthritis that typically accompanies giantism finally crippled her a few months before her death in 1888. The front door of her house, along with a part of the side paneling, had to be removed in order to get the eight-foot long casket out of the house on rollers. Sixteen pallbearers couldn't lift it. She was buried in the Weld Street Cemetery in Wilton, but was moved later to Lakeview overlooking Wilson Pond. It was said that the reason she was moved was because some of her Spiritualist friends heard she wasn't resting comfortably.

Surprisingly, there is little mention in Sylvia's history of the taunting to which she must have been subject. A contemporary historian, John Haven Willard, writing in *The Maine Farmer* in 1867, mentions a man unexpectedly encountering Sylvia on a sidewalk in Wilton and leaping six or eight feet sideways in amazement. Blanche Applebee tells a story she heard from George Goding, the boarder: It seems a traveling salesman was staying in Sylvia's house one night and began to make remarks about her size. While the other boarders tried to sidetrack the conversation, the city slicker wouldn't leave her alone. Finally Sylvia, who had been ignoring the man, reached across the table, lifted him straight out of his seat, and then slammed him back down through the cane bottom, all without saying a word.

Another popular story is of a time when Sylvia was working in a farmer's home. While carrying two full quart milk pans into the house, she got her hair caught on an iron hook that hung from the ceiling. Unable to set the milk down to free herself, she called for help. The farmer came, but delayed freeing her while he called others to come and see her fantastic predicament, whereupon Sylvia poured the contents of both milk pans over his head.

If the reaction of others to her was unusual, so too was the manner in which she lived. In her house on Depot Street the shades started six to eight inches below the tops of the windows so she could see out above them. She kept her looking glass and hair brush on the top ledges of the windows, alongside photos tacked to the ceiling of her friends from the Barnum days. When she left the show, Barnum had given her a gold watch that measured five inches in diameter, the size of a tea saucer. It was said that a ring she wore was big enough to serve as a child's bracelet. Neighbors reported that her windows were decorated with black cats, in keeping with her Spiritualist beliefs.

Apparently her Barnum years (no one, not even the Circus World Museum Library in Baraboo, Wisconsin, knows how long she appeared with his show) were the happiest years of her life. Having been thrown together with other people of extraordinary proportions or features, she found in some sense her peers and made perhaps her only true friends. A photo album (since lost) containing pictures and postcards of the other sideshow performers was one of her cherished possessions, and each card was signed with a token of affection for Sylvia. These friends included the India Rubber Man, the Wild Men of Borneo, the Living Skeleton, the Bearded Lady and her son the Dog-Faced Boy, the Siamese Twins, and of course, General and Mrs. Tom Thumb. Her favorite photo was from Mrs. Thumb, which was inscribed, "To my best friend, Sylvia, from her best friend, Lavinia."

Friends must have been exceptionally important to her; it takes little imagination to see that hers was a life of great loneliness. Her predecessor as Tallest Lady in the World, Anna Swan, married another giant, Captain Martin Van Buren Bates (making them the World's Tallest Husband and Wife). But Sylvia had no such companion. Indeed, her mother's wish was to outlive Sylvia, presumably to provide her with companionship. She just barely made it: Jane Hardy Leonard died two weeks after her daughter.

To describe a giant, we emphasize the grand details: the head brushing the ceiling, the spread hands that could cover a newspaper, the difficulties of living in an ordinary-sized world. To describe a person, we need the more modest details of character.

It is these small details that are missing from Sylvia's story. Those that survive suggest a kind and average person trapped in a body that must have seemed a cruel mistake. She was said to be a good cook; she grew flowers, visited neighbors, and went for long walks in the woods and fields. She used to fashion doll's clothes and bonnets for neighborhood children and swap posies with their mothers. Sometimes she would pick her flowers and pass them out to the children passing by on their way to school.

Comments that describe her as other than a giant or a Spiritualist are rare and not very helpful. Her "eyes were as black as soot," said one; "she had thick, black hair," remarked another. Several people mentioned that she was masculine-looking, with a deep voice. A woman who sang at her funeral remembered that she "talked very intelligently." The Portland *Argus* disputed the color of her eyes, saying they were blue, but otherwise noted that "her complexion was fair . . . and the very modest and mild expression of her countenance is said to be the index of her character."

As she grew helplessly from the rather attractive young woman with the scarf in her hair to the acromegalic giant whose eyes sunk into the flesh of her face, she must have come to see it as a punishment. It isn't too much to imagine that her fascination with the spirit world, and with her own death (her coffin had been ready for ten years by the time she died), suggest a hope for a better world, or at least a different one, in which she'd be free of the sentence of her size. Perhaps the best indication of how she felt about her life as a giant is the brief inscription she ordered for her tombstone. She had once been famous as the Maine Giantess and the Tallest Lady in the World. But on her gravestone there is only the simple message: "Sylvia Hardy. Died August 25, 1888. Aged 65."

Social Radio
(2020)

Every weekday, three times a day, our local radio station here in western Maine pauses in its parade of Top 40 hits. Peppy electronic sounds begin, leading to ten minutes of something called "PhoneMart." I'm not sure how you spell it but Phone Mart, or Phonemart, should be studied by anthropologists for the insight it provides into humanity, economics, and the availability of snowplow blades. Phone Mart is social media, but not that social media.

During Phone Mart people call in to offer things to sell, or to buy; to ask for services, or to provide services. The Phone Mart doesn't involve typing, you can't do it on your computer, and you actually have to call in or listen to someone in real time.

Mostly it goes like this: On a day in early January, a guy calls to offer to sell his 2009 Silverado equipped with a straight plow, a truck that is "loaded" and is "a big boy truck," he says. Someone else has a 27 inch Panasonic TV, free. The next person says he'll shovel snow off roofs. A tattooing kit, unopened, is offered; good price, twenty dollars. Another man wants to talk about the weather before he gets to his business. Another describes his car as "clean as a smelt." There is only one woman-caller in this segment, who is selling firewood: "cut, split, and delivered," the three verbs a chant of sorts around here.

When there is a lag between calls, the disc jockey will read Public Service Announcements, updating listeners on cancellations (the wrestling meet for the local high school is still on), reminding us that the Masons are having a public lunch the following day where pork will be served, following up with an announcement about a substance abuse clinic.

The calls rattle on swiftly, until someone goes off script, wanting to chat up the d.j. Phone Mart sometimes dabbles in ethics: One woman calls just to say "bring your pets in" before a nasty stretch of January weather. Once, someone wanted to sell guns and the d.j. had to cut him off—no guns for sale on Phone Mart, and no callers allowed from out of the broadcast area.

And sometimes Phone Mart provides another type of service, the service of being heard. An elderly woman dialed in just before Valentine's Day one year. The disc jockey answered the call in the usual manner, with "You're on KTJ's Phone Mart," and in a thin, cracking voice she slowly said, "I'd like to get a Valentine's card this year."

The d.j. gamely carried on, despite the twist in the formula: "You would, would you?"

"Yes, I'm a lonely old woman and I'd like to have someone love me on Valentine's Day." Her voice dripped with sadness.

"Well, we'll see what we can do. Maybe one of our listeners can help you out there. What's your number?" he asked. Then, "Can anyone get a Valentines' card for that lady?" I like to think someone did.

Listen long enough and you get a vision of your neighbor's lives. A man calls in a quiet, soft voice, asking if anyone has a small dinette set for sale. I picture him, lonely in a tiny kitchen. There is the man who calls in to wish everyone a Merry Christmas; the person who calls day after day, every session, offering the same used television for five dollars.

Recently, I tried to give away a camp refrigerator, listing it on a well-known online forum; like usual, I got trolled by a few of those odd, anonymous people who spend their time doing such things. I gave up and called Phone Mart. I had two calls in five minutes and the refrigerator was gone the next day to a local church.

Life in rural Maine can sometimes seem relentlessly provincial; we are a backwater, an eddy in the stream of contemporary society. The Phone Mart is one of our provincial institutions, defiantly unhip, yet for decades connecting the thrifty, the lonely, the poor to one another. And to those needing a tattoo kit.

Requiem For A Maple
(2020)

It was the first maple I tapped for maple sap, in 1988, the second year of our lives in Maine; a grand old tree with spreading branches that reached probably forty feet in every direction, north to south and east to west. The house, built in the mid-1860s, came after the tree, and the tree asserted itself by spreading its branches so far they touched the corner of the house where the roof line joined the eaves, providing a launching pad for squirrels to leap from tree to roof and then into the attic.

I forgave the tree, got rid of the squirrels, cut the branches back. Some tapping seasons I hung three buckets from the tree, and as the years went by, and it started to show its age, just one, and then none. It was a "yard tree" in the language of maple syrup makers, producing sweeter sap than maples deeper in the grove. Some of the bigger branches died, and smaller branches would sheer off in a winter wind. Then two winters ago, the tree split in a ferocious windstorm and the eastern half came down in a roar, pointing directly at but not reaching our road.

The tree was too big for me to handle with my chain saw, and my wife wouldn't let me saw it up anyhow, recognizing my limitations as an arborist-professor better than I did. Months passed, it was now June, and one morning while my wife and I were working in our respective home offices, a sound started, a sound you don't hear very often, a long whoosh, like a giant broom being swept through the sky, then my wife yelling, then wood splintering and the house shaking.

I rushed downstairs. Checked the wife: unharmed but upset; checked the windows: none broken; looked outside: another huge section of the maple filled the yard, having fallen directly along the front of the house, parallel to it and perpendicular to where the first half of the tree had fallen, and just brushing, but not pulling down, the power line to the house.

I got one of our local tree experts to come out and finish taking down the rest of the tree, and he and his helper cut the trunk up into sixteen-inch pieces, some of which I broke up with a splitter for firewood that year. But I had him save two very large branches of the tree, one about nine feet long, the other six, and each about twelve inches in diameter.

The tree had shaded the house, provided maple sap, been a sentinel, the kind of large maple tree you want to have in your yard when you move to Maine. It had nearly crushed the house, but it was an old maple. Worthy of my respect. When you have lived in the same house for a long time, especially in an old house—built well before you were born—you develop a sense of loyalty to the entire place, a feeling of obligation. You have temporarily been entrusted with its care; others before you cared for it, others after you will hopefully do the same. Having been nurtured by and nurtured the place, you are in a relation-ship with it, one that has to be taken seriously. In short, I owed the tree.

So I decided I would convert it into something other than BTUs. I would save it, after a fashion. And the only way I could think of to do that was to make boards out of the rescued limbs, and someday, some distant day, do something with those boards.

There were a few problems: I didn't have a saw mill to turn the wood into slabs, or a planer to smooth them into useable boards, or a good way of moving them to a place where these things could be done. However, I did have a bad way to move them: in late fall last year I backed our old pickup truck next to where the logs were. They were too heavy to lift, even after volunteering my wife to help with the lifting, which she is always gamely willing to do.

I got various pieces of lumber scraps, used them to build a ramp from the ground to the tailgate of my pickup. But the logs were still on the ground, not on the ramp. Then I took a four-foot long piece of flat steel, used for another project some years before—fulcruming up one corner of our barn—rolled one of the rescued branches onto the steel, placed some of the smaller stump pieces of the tree on either side of the log, then lifted one end of the steel and placed it on a stump, then went around to the other side and lifted the other end of the steel and put it on another stump. Archimedes would have been proud.

Going back and forth in this way I was able to lift the end of the log higher to where it now could rest on the ramp to the pickup. Then I got an old nylon strap, used for tying down loads on a truck, and my come-along winch. I secured the strap around the log, hooked one end of the come-along to the strap, and hooked the other end to the front of the pickup bed, the idea being that I could winch the log up the ramp, onto the bed of the truck.

My wife came out to provide grudging support; actually, what she said, was, "You'll kill us both." As I ratcheted the come-along, she kept the log centered on the ramp. The log began to move, to make the slow journey up the ramp. The wire of the come-along grew taut, then tight, and each pull on the ratchet became more and more difficult. But the log still inched up the ramp.

And then the strap broke, sending the come-along whizzing

through the air, right between our heads, smashing the rear window of the pickup. Glass fell into the pickup bed, the log fell off the ramp, my wife gave me a look.

But this country wasn't built by people who were intimidated by hard work; it was built by people who hired other people to do the hard work, people who knew what they were doing.

I called Mark, the man I had contacted earlier who was prepared to saw the log into boards, and explained the problem. It wasn't a problem for him. He'd caught the spirit of the thing, or at least pretended to. Not long before Christmas he brought over a trailer with an electric winch, ran a cable through what was now a snowy yard, hooked it to the log, and dragged it across the snow and into his trailer and was off. Thirty minutes, tops.

A week or so later Mark called to say he was ready to cut up the logs, and did I want to watch? On a cold January day I drove over to his place in East Dixfield and watched him turn the logs into inch-and-a-half thick slabs. The portable saw was awesome, just the kind of machine a man would find fascinating, and it made fast work of the logs. I stacked the slabs in the back of the pickup, whose rear window was now cardboard and duct tape, and drove them home. I cut six-inch long pieces of pine into inch-square posts, to "stick" the slabs, putting two or three of these posts between each slab, to allow for air to move around them, to help with the drying after I stacked them in a corner of the barn. Finally, I took ropes and wrapped the stack and pulled tight, to keep the boards from warping. Then I let them sit all winter, all mud season, all spring, and in mid-summer I was ready for the next step.

I found a carpenter, Wes, out in Fayette, who will plane them smooth for me and then they will be these beautiful, eccentric objects, mine to do with what I will. The best part is I have no particular use for them, no project in mind. I never did, and still don't. I just wanted to honor our old maple, by turning it into a lasting testament to old trees and obligations. A pointless alchemy, really, which so far has cost me $350 for sixteen boards, most of that for the truck window. Totally worth it.

Four

The Ends

This final section has a simple logic to it: These two are the longest and shortest pieces in the collection, and in a way they have to do with endings. They also represent two of the types of pieces I love to write: the segmented essay, in episodic form, where I am able to catalogue a list of experiences and details; and the short, epiphanic (when I'm lucky) essay, which takes a small moment and does something worthwhile (maybe) with it.

Maine country fairs are particularly fruitful territory for the collection approach: they are both familiar and strange, strange, strange, and paying attention to the strangeness while at the same time documenting the familiar pleases me, and hopefully others. And, an experience like being the commencement speaker for a high school graduating class of 11 students, in a tiny town (the Switzerland of Maine!), is a delicious one for a writer. Even headed to the event, driving up through north-west Maine towards the border with Quebec, I knew there was an essay coming. That's the thrill for the writer, sometimes, if "thrill" isn't too strong a word: to know you've got material and now you are waiting to see what you'll make of it; you stand outside yourself, watching to see what you're capable of, what will come out, what the result will be. It's almost exciting, to be divided in this way, witnessing and doing.

Both appeared in *Down East*, in 2009 and 2011, respectively.

A Fair Season
(2011)

"The Fair only comes once a year."

Mr. Arable, *Charlotte's Web*

A small crowd has gathered around an open air stall in the animal section of the Blue Hill Fair in late August. It is the kind of gathering that pulls other people to it, as everyone is staring at the same thing. I stop at the fringe and peer over the heads. We are all looking at a large buff cow, lying on her side, rear towards us, out of which a hoof protrudes.

People are quiet, whispering even, as we watch the birth of the calf here at the Fair. Who knew there would be calf birthing at the Fair, as though it was another exhibit, among the displays of chickens, rabbits, pigs, horses, oxen, steer, lambs? In another half hour the crowd will double, and the calf will now be a hoof and a leg, and the cow will moo loudly sometimes, sometimes moan low, and we will all be moved by the sight, by the sound, by the experience of a public birth.

It's all here at the Fair! Everything's here at the Fair. The Fair is a universe, as rich as a forest in diversity and relationships, more colorful than any art museum, more variety than an entire city, epic in its scope!

Yet I have had a vexed relationship with Maine Fairs since I came to the state years ago. Sometimes I think Fairs in Maine say something essential about the state, and I am taken by the charms of them; at other times they seem merely seedy and tacky, and representative of nothing so much as of rural poverty and of a desire to cling to a vanished past.

That is where one might find oneself when one stands outside the Fair experience. But one summer I crawled inside the Fair experience, immersed myself in it, gave it a full chance; in short, I tried to see how much Fair food I could absorb and survive.

I discovered that the state of Maine actually maintains a website devoted to Maine Fairs, or "Maine Agricultural Fairs," as they are officially known. There I found 25 Fairs listed, in chronological order, from July 3rd in Houlton, to the official closing of Fair season at Fryeburg, on the first weekend of October. There was a "World's Fair" (Waterford), a "State Fair" (Bangor), and a "Free Fair" (in the town and condition of Harmony). Only the last was titled accurately.

I set myself the task of visiting as many as possible. I made it to almost half, drove nearly to California without leaving the borders of Maine, spent more than a month doing it, saw many things I'd never seen before or even imagined, and at times felt as though I had crossed that border between being a visitor to the Fair and part of the Fair itself. One wonders such things as why there are so many Fairs in Maine, more than New Hampshire, more than Vermont (one Fair for every 52,000 residents, roughly), what they represent to us, what they say about us, and why there is such a fascination with large animals pulling heavy objects. And I asked myself, How is each Fair unique, In what aspects are they all the same?

The former was harder to identify than the latter, but still, picking out the <u>one</u> thing that every single Fair has, and which every Fair in the region and maybe the nation has, was a challenge. But at last, at the end of the season, after much labor, I discovered what that was.

Entering the Fair begins long before you enter the Fair. Fairs in Maine wisely don't begin until about the Fourth of July, mirroring the fact that summer doesn't start in Maine until the 4th, if then. Driving to the Fair is your first experience of it. For example, driving to the Blue Hill Fair in late August, I begin seeing signs for the Fair miles in advance, stuck to telephone poles along Routes 1 and 3, then Route 15. A different time, driving to Harmony for their Fair, I see things I've never seen: a vista from the top of a rise near Solon, a tiny township (Concord) I didn't know existed, communities which awaken that ancient impulse to wonder, How do they live here? What do they do to survive? What is winter like in a place like this? I also come to an intersection where several boards are hammered to posts, declaring "Impeach Them All." These are the things you see when you approach the Fair. And then you arrive.

All Fairs announce themselves by the cluster of cars on the sides of the road. All Fairs have parking areas that are large grass and mud fields, with volunteers wearing colorful smocks and waving flags on the end of sticks to direct the traffic into the lot. License plates say a great deal about a Fair: Some Fairs have license plates from everywhere—New Jersey, Virginia, Florida, Massachusetts, Connecticut, North Carolina, Pennsylvania, Vermont, up and down the eastern seaboard—and a few don't have a single out of state plate.

Many of the same pieces and parts are at all Fairs: these include the ticket booth, the midway with rides and games, food stands, the animal exhibition, a pulling hall or corral, a demonstration area, and perhaps a racetrack. Almost all have a place for a demolition derby, a bandstand, and some make space for tractor pulling as well.

The Fair can be distilled to this, and there is in fact one Fair that captures that distilled version of Fair.

One can't resist the lure of a Fair in a place called "Harmony," particularly as it is the Harmony Free Fair, three of the most attractive words there are. The Harmony Free Fair is held in early September, in that period embracing Labor Day weekend when there is a cluster of Fairs (Blue Hill, Springfield, and Windsor). No signs are posted directing you to this Fair, because everyone who is going to it already knows where it is, hidden in a valley where a cluster of roads come together. I had taken "free" to be a testament to some sort of community value, the same spirit that caused towns in Maine to be named Unity, Freedom, Albion, Athens, and Hope, but it turned out "free" meant, well, free: no cost.

Therefore, Harmony dispensed with the ticket booth; one just crosses the street from the parking area in the field next to the elementary school, and walks along a broad path, up hill and into the Fairgrounds. Instantly you are in the "midway": Four rides, all of them the air-filled, birthday-party type, a half dozen food stands, and three games. To the left is the demolition derby pit, which has here been reduced to as small a space as possible, and still allow for this strange occupation. It is a pit of 75 yards by 25 yards, fenced-in by road construction barriers. The area is so small it is probably not possible to get up much of a head of steam inside, which must make for a tame demolition.

To the right, the south, is the rest of the Fair. First, a bandstand, a portable trailer whose long side lifts up and can be propped open. There are two or three partially-filled bleachers arrayed in a half circle around the bandstand, spottily filled. Further to the south are local food stands, including the Wellington

Volunteer Fire Department affair. Uphill from there, to the east, is where animals are exhibited. At Harmony the animal exhibit was a tiny three-walled shed with three or four cows, two calves, and a tired looking pony, and that was it.

Furthest south is the demonstration area. All demonstration areas must have, it seems, at least three things: someone chopping wood in one fashion or another; a blacksmith shop; and antique engines. The antique engines were at every single Fair, and they are so organized they even have their own website. Downhill from the demonstration area, over a small bluff, were a series of horseshoe pits, about a dozen, all in use; the horseshoe competition part of Harmony had begun.

I sit for a time in the one set of wooden, rickety bleachers above the demolition derby pit. I'm glad I didn't see the derby; it would have been too atonal for Harmony. I go watch the blacksmith demonstration, have a hamburger made specially for me at the Patriarch Club booth, capture napkins that blow away thanks to the wind coming from Canada, watch the wood-cutting demonstration, the antique engine set-up, a horse dressage competition for youngsters dressed in their western best, taking their horses on a slow, careful ride around the corral; watch a display of weaving, look at the sad little animal display, and walk up and down the "midway," which takes me but three minutes to traverse, even while strolling. I listen for a while to the local band, "Miles to Go" which features a thin female singer, a bass player, drummer and guitarist. Like most local bands, they aren't bad, as long as they stick to what they have played a hundred times before. No one is dancing, but people are attentive and applaud at the right moments.

I somehow miss the Women's Skillet Tossing contest, and the parade. I particularly regret the parade, as the village of Harmony is only a few hundred yards long, and I would have liked to see what kind of parade could do justice to that space.

In Harmony everyone knows everyone else, and therefore I

am greeted heartily, both as I enter and leave the Fair. It is a lovely day, a bit windy, not too hot, just a lovely day to spend at a Fair.

Maine even has a Fair Coordinator, an official state position, listed right there on the State of Maine government website. His name is Fred Lunt, Jr, which somehow seems like the perfect name for a Fair commissioner in its crisp simplicity.

I meet Fred Lunt on a dismal fall day, rainy and raw and foreshadowing winter, a few weeks after Fair season has ended, and when he has finally returned to his office after three months on the road, or rather, three months at the Fair. Fred's office is in the old Augusta Mental Health Institute building, which is not a comment on what kind of person will spend three months bouncing from Fair to Fair. For those three months Fred lives in a Department of Agriculture trailer that is towed around the state and set up at the larger Fairs. He lives in the front quarter of the trailer; the back three-fourths are displays, promoting agriculture in Maine.

Fred is 59, a bit shorter than average, with a friendly if measured way of speaking. He comes originally from Presque Isle and from a background in farming and agriculture, and has been involved in Fairs for more than 30 years. For the last eleven he has been the Fair Commissioner, but before that he was the Fair Manager in Skowhegan, and then Clinton, where he now lives. He is a man who knows his Fairs.

One thing I want to know from Fred is, What is the point of a Fair? and, Why does Maine have so many?

"Well you know they grew out of the Grange," he says. Really? I say. I had no idea. "Yes, the local Granges were the ones who first put on Fairs, to display their local animals and produce and crafts. Maine probably has more Fairs than other states, because the Granges stayed a little stronger over time.

"Now the Fairs are both exhibitions and educational," Fred continues. "They're not just to display their agriculture products, but also to encourage people to get involved too, and explain to them how to do the crafts, the farming, whatever."

Okay, but this still doesn't explain blooming onions and the ride known as the Zipper.

I ask Fred whether Fairs are a dying part of the Maine cultural landscape and he says emphatically no. "We've added a couple in the years I've been in this job, and a couple of places are trying to bring back old Fairs. So, no, they aren't dying out at all." Indeed, by the end of World War Two, an odd paradox developed in Maine and throughout New England, where farm populations dwindled while attendance at Fairs rose. It is a paradox that continues: farm populations dwindle, fair attendance increases, as though there is an inverse and necessary relationship to one another.

Agricultural Fairs were a successor to the commercial Fairs that have existed for centuries. Beginning in the mid-1800s the commercial Fair gave way to the agricultural Fair, and, as one history of Agricultural Fairs notes, they in turn incorporated "popular entertainment that had attracted peasants to the old markets." In 1810, the progenitor of the modern Fair began in Berkshire County, Massachusetts. Post Civil-War, Fairs changed again when the Grange (also known as the Order of the Patrons of Husbandry) claimed that Fairs "had grown frivolous and corrupt." Grangers started their own Fairs, but discovered that they needed "horse races and side shows" in order to attract an audience. Modern Granges still "try to recruit members and remind people that Fairs, despite their current diversity, have primary ties to the land." The tension between "pure" agricultural Fairs and "popular" exhibitions continues, though mostly it is a happy marriage.

The Windsor Fair is actually in South Windsor, which is a perfect metaphor for much of the Fair experience, where things are not always exactly as they appear.

Windsor is my first large, traditional Fair, and it is a bit over-whelming. There are so many people, more people than one normally finds gathered together in one place in Maine. I try to define the Fair crowd: they are dressed casually, certainly, and they are overwhelmingly white, but what else? One thing I notice is that everyone is grouped in couples or families or gangs of teenagers, but few singles. It appears going to the Fair is a communal activity. Lots of dyed hair, shaved hair, ripped jeans, dyed jeans, tattoos, piercings, chains, but also flannel, the "Maine Apple Princess" banner on a girl, green Dickie pants (the official uniform of the retired male Mainer), the flushed red face of an alcoholic, the smooth dark skin of the Hispanic workers who set up and run many of the rides, and one t-shirt that says "God so loved the world that he gave it Grandmothers."

I decide I will be rigorous at Windsor, tackle it in an orderly fashion. From the front gate I turn quickly into a long shed displaying vegetables and crafts. There are quilts, garlic, green tomatoes, banzai trees. The floor is polished wood, that kind of polish that comes from thousands of shoes over dozens of years. At first it seems merely to be a long shed displaying vegetables and crafts, but then I notice the ribbons, hundreds of ribbons, ribbons on every single item. I stop to look at one: it is a First Place, but I don't know for what until I search further and find a thin cardboard tab that lists the name of the owner, the category and sub-category, and the address and phone number, so then I know that Meredith Baker has placed First in the category of "Tomatoes, Plum" in the 2008 Windsor County Fair. I look at the tomato: it is starting to slump on to its plate, and has sprung some cracks, and may be leaking a little juice, and I'm wondering how long it has been here, and what Second Place looks like.

From vegetables I head to history and antique farm implements. This is always an important part of a Fair, as it is the past which Fairs celebrate, and secondarily the present, but only in so far as the present invokes and continues the noble past.

There is a barn full of farm equipment, including a thresher, a hay wagon, a one horsepower Johnson outboard motor with a pull start. All of the people in the museum are old enough to have once used the harrow, the thresher, which hints at the absence of the future at the Fair. There is a ghostly sound inside the old wooden building; it is the sound of traffic passing by outside, on Route 32, the present trying to intrude on those of us here in the past.

From there I venture to the old schoolhouse. Farmington has such a display, so does Fryeburg and Oxford. An old schoolhouse marks the dividing line between a Fair and a major Fair. There are other such markers, like tractor pulling, permanent exhibition halls, and horseracing, but with schoolhouses the idea is that you step inside and you step into the past, and you are to marvel at the simplicity of the building, the stern features, and appreciate how hard children had it then, how basic and even primitive going to school was, and what sterling character this must have produced.

I always have the wrong reaction: the buildings are made of weathered old wood, the woodstove in the center of the room—meant to suggest how cold the students must have been—looks cozy, and the old-fashioned slate chalkboard looks perfectly usable. The Shaker pegs where coats and gloves were hung are exactly like the ones I have in my house, and the simple wooden desks and chairs don't seem any more uncomfortable than the ones college students sit in now. And the schoolhouse has granite footings and white-washed clapboards and the effect is further ruined for me by my belief that there is nothing prettier than Maine granite and clapboards in late afternoon light.

This past and present tension is everywhere in the Fair: are we in the past, or are we in the present? Usually it is clear: the rides are now, the Fairgrounds are yesterday, the food is current, the barns are the past, and so on. Anything that smacks of the future is banished. On some level this might be troubling, as it suggests Maine has no future, or doesn't know what that future might be. Fairs don't do Futures; there isn't a hint, even a whiff, of the future at any Maine Fair, with the possible exception of some of the rides, which hope to invoke space travel: the Gravit-ron, for instance. The absence of Future is something to consider while at a Fair, but I don't let it trouble me today, and wander on.

There is a sugarhouse, as there will be at Oxford, Farming-ton, Fryeburg, the grand Fairs. Inside the model sap house an evaporator sends up clouds of steam, although it is just water that is boiling, not sap. Maple products are for sale, including maple candy, maple popcorn, maple cream, maple syrup, and maple leafs. There are handbooks on how to make maple syrup, and photos of maple syrup operations around the walls, which are made of the same rough-cut lumber from which many real sugar houses are made. The photos are mostly black and white, in keeping with the imagery of the past, although they are mod-ern photographs, taken recently. The sugarhouses at every Fair are always crowded, partly because it takes several people to run the house, but also because they are popular. There is a desire—especially among the male population—to imagine that one will give up one's boring, ordinary life and become the owner of a sugarbush—a romantic notion, usually doomed, crushed by the realities of 21st century life.

Having moved around the eastern and northern portions of the Fair, I am spit out into the center of it, the midway and food. It is late afternoon and the walkways are packed with people ei-ther searching out rides or food. I settle for food. The problem is, which booth to frequent? So many choices, and the choices forming a chant.

French fries, curly fries, fried dough, fried scallops, fried chicken fingers, fried clams, clam chowder, lobster roll, ice cream, hot dogs, hamburgers, gyros, cotton candy, candy apples, roasted nuts, blooming onions, onion rings, apple crisp, baked potatoes, stuffed potatoes, thai noodles, funnel cake, pork wings, whoopee pies, vegetable soup, baked beans, corn chowder, Italian sausage, kielbasa, falafel, lemonade, steak, kettle corn.

But which one captures the essence of Fair? I can get a burger anywhere, and I can't see eating a blooming onion for dinner, and I refuse to buy anything from a stand whose sign reads "French Frie's." Thai food doesn't shout "Fair" to me, although it looks good. No, it must be something that one can only get at such a bacchanalian place, at a Fair. And that is onion rings, Moxie, and a red hot dog.

I pay for my treasure and find an open spot among the tables in a picnic area across from the food booths. The tables are filled with families and older couples, and wheelchairs, and oxygen tanks. Everyone is welcome at the Fair, no matter what condition.

There is nothing like Fair food. Fair food is food you would never eat on your own, at any other time or in any other location. No doubt Fair food drives health officials mad, for it invariably involves grease, and no "heart healthy" types of oil. Between the grease, the fat, the meat, the reused grease, the fat, the oil, the sweets that rival the grease, Fair food is an exercise in blissful mass suicide.

What makes a perfectly healthy, normal person with good eating habits eat Fair food? The smell. You are walking around the Fair, minding your own business, when you realize there is this smell, this allure, in the air. It is probably the smell of meat frying in grease, and even though you are a vegetarian and avoid butter, salt, oils made from coconut or palm, and even though you ate only an hour ago, you suddenly start thinking of how you'd like to eat something, anything.

So you seek out the fried onion rings, the blooming onion,

the French fries, the fried whoopee pie, and the lemonade to wash it down, or the frostee, ice cream, fried ice cream, root beer, or at Litchfield Fair, "Kajun Kevin's Home Brew." After eating at the Fair one feels that is the end of eating, that one will never take pleasure in food ever again. Until the next Fair, when the smells will overwhelm you again.

I'm not sure about the permanent effect on my internal organs of any of my Fair meals, but the only thing I truly regretted was a kielbasa. I didn't think I'd ever had a kielbasa before and thought I should—in the interest of the investigation—try one out, but I could only stomach a few bites before I ended the experiment.

Meanwhile, back at Windsor and my dinner, I finish my onion rings, and drain my Moxie—a tart drink which inspires disgust or loyalty, and which should only be drunk at a Fair—before plunging back in again.

I come upon a cow-milking contest, with a twist. The cow milkers are local politicians, Maine State legislators. The politicians may be good at milking taxpayers—which is perhaps the underlying joke here—but not so good at cows. It is hard to say what the purpose of this event is supposed to be: public humiliation of the elected officials? A chance for them to demonstrate what ordinary citizens they are (but what ordinary citizen knows how to milk a cow?), or for those who know how to milk, to demonstrate their superiority over those who do not? The politicians get on their stools, after being instructed on which side of the cow to sit, shown the basic gesture (pull and squeeze, or squeeze and pull), and the contest begins. A commentator with a microphone keeps a running narrative going while they milk. "There you go, Representative X, you've got the right idea, but Senator Y is ahead of you. Careful Ms. Z, you're spraying the milk all over—the idea is to get it in the pail, you know." Their supporters—some dressed in t-shirts upon which their candidates names is emblazoned—cheer them on, sometimes more mocking than cheering.

Mockery is on my mind, because it is so easy to mock all of this, as I continue my tour; not just the clumsy cow milkers, but to stand outside of the Fair and see it as corny, cheap, a cliché. But the longer you stay at the Fair, somehow, gradually, the distance begins to fall away and one begins to participate, to lose that self-consciousness that people like me bring to the Fairgrounds. I play two hands of Bingo in the Bingo tent; don't come even close to winning. As I leave, the setting sun is lighting up the bandstand where a concert is about to begin. Cotton-candy clouds, an image inspired by Fair food, hover over the bandstand. The slightest chill is creeping into the air, but for now it is still summer and it is still Fair season in Maine.

What spot do demolition derbies occupy in the national psyche? Are they Roller Derby for cars? Are they like professional wrestling, not quite real yet still jarring? Are they kitsch, does no one take them seriously?

It is hard to know. I saw two that summer; one was deadly serious and the other rather self-conscious. The first was at the North New Portland Fair, hosted by the local Lions Club. North New Portland's Fair is short, held Friday to Sunday, as are a few of the other Fairs (the pattern is three-day Fairs, then four-day, then week-long). When I arrived on Sunday about noon, the ticket-taker at the entrance to the Fairground (off Route 27, on Route 146, past the Katie Crotch Road, many twists and turns) had given up, because of the heavy rains: in fact, that's what he said, "I give up" when I pulled next to the booth to pay my entrance fee, and he waved me through without taking it. "It's a disaster," he shouted as I drove past, which seemed a little extreme, given that there was still a small crowd in the muddy Fairgrounds.

Most of that crowd was headed towards the demolition derby pit, which was bordered by a sloping hill upon which people had spread blankets and chairs to witness the spectacle. Around three sides of the derby pit pickups backed up, tailgates let down and spectators prepared themselves with raincoats and blankets and picnic baskets. On the fourth side, where the cars would enter, was an announcers' booth on stilts. Beneath the booth the drivers were gathered together by the race Director, Buster Pinkham, who read the rules to them. The drivers included two women, I noticed, which was a heartening sight, that women could participate on an equal footing with men in the destruction of cars. I take note of the fact that the demotion derby is being partially sponsored by a local chiropractor. Ironic, and perhaps a savvy bit of market creation.

Having been instructed, the drivers returned to their cars and the first round of ten entered the ring, with two rows of five arranged across from each other, each row facing towards the outside of the ring. Then, surprisingly, the drivers were told to turn their engines off and the pit fell silent. Very dramatic. Two older women in white pants and black blouses stepped carefully through the mud and up into the announcing booth. A cappella, they sang the National Anthem while the rest of us stood respectfully.

I couldn't figure out at first why the cars in North New Portland were arrayed with their rears facing each other, and why this was the way they pursued each other, but it quickly became obvious: hitting with the front would soon destroy the engine, and then—tragically—you would have lost the derby.

The derby began at the shrill sound of a horn and the cars burped into action. Motors roaring, tires screaming, mud flying, they backed into each other and soon smoke began to fill the air, and I noticed the local volunteer firemen in place with their hoses already out. Some drivers wore helmets, some didn't. The oily smoke started to obscure the scene, and one wondered if engines ever caught on fire, but then of course the firemen and fire trucks are there for a reason, so probably yes. The entire scene is beyond satire, too bizarre to require commentary—nothing could heighten the absurdity of people destroying automotive vehicles for no good reason, other than the thrill. When I think of what ingenuity went into the creating of the automobile, and how many resources and how much infrastructure was required to get these ten cars here, to this spot in North New Portland, Maine, to this wanton destruction, I am amazed at the sheer waste, sheer profligacy of this event. "Derby" is far too genteel a name for all of this.

It is also great fun, to watch the cars slam and jerk around. Just then an old sedan smashes into the side of a station wagon and the tire of the wagon falls off. It can no longer move, so the driver just sits inside and waits for the mayhem to end.

In the second heat of ten, two of the drivers get into a fight and are tossed out of the competition in mid-duel. What could possibly prompt anger at a demolition, when the whole purpose is to destroy each other's cars anyhow? What honor has been tromped upon, what rule—unwritten or written—has been violated? In any case, the two drivers stomp away and one of them soon leaves the Fair, packing his ruined car onto a tow truck and driving off. I ask Buster about this. "Oh," he says, "that wasn't just something that happened here. Those boys had something going from before."

My second demolition derby, at Farmington, was held in the infield area of the race track, witnessed from the grandstand, under a full moon loitering above. Like the derby in North New Portland, this pit was bordered by cement barriers and big rocks, with an opening through which the knights of the joust entered, and then were pulled out—crippled and defeated—later.

Quickly, several cars were turned in to squashed metal bugs by a direct hit and an unfortunate crumpling of metal. Soon the contest was down to three vehicles, one of which could move only slowly, and the other two raced around this one, pursuing each other, one moving in reverse, the other chasing going forward.

Around and around the two raced, while the third car crept out of their way. The announcer screamed through the loud-speaker system, narrating the action, and while the driving seemed more professional than at North New Portland, clearly the crowd here had a more wry view on the activity. The announcers in particular were a treat. There were two, as though one was doing the color commentary at a football game. One of them said "It's like a ballet out there," and then later that he was only "being rhetorical."

If demolition derbies are not the part of Fair culture that would be most puzzling to someone from, say, Afghanistan, or at least someone from Miami, then truck pulls would have to be. I had at least seen a demolition derby or two before I began my pilgrimage that summer, but I'd never even heard of a tractor pull before I showed up at the Clinton Fair on a gray day in August.

A parking attendant directed me to a spot in the obligatory broad, slightly muddy parking field. When I left the car, I heard a roar a short distance away, the loudest sound I'd ever heard at a Fair. Obviously mechanical, the sound was angry and desperate, at the end of its abilities, unable to roar any louder or fiercer. This was hard to resist, so I walked down the row of cars to a big crowd. The crowd seemed to be all men, and many of them were holding beers. It was about 1 o'clock in the afternoon, so this was something new: early drinking, at the Fair, accompanied by metallic shrieks.

I was at the back of a set of bleachers, and had to wiggle through the beer drinkers to get to the front, to a chain-link fence where I could see what was going on. A pickup truck, motor shrieking, front wheels in the air and huge rear wheels spitting up dirt, was attempting to pull a bizarre machine from my left to right. The sight of the truck straining in agony at its task was weird enough, but weirder was the thing it was attempting to pull. This was a long, flat vehicle, with wheels, and with a sort of pilot house on the back end. It was chained to the competing truck, which had now given up, the front wheels dropping to the ground, the engine reduced to an idle. Someone came out and marked the spot where the strange thing being pulled had stopped. On the side of the pulled thing was stenciled "Northern Penobscot Truck Puller Association," which implied that this was an official activity, something sanctioned and organized by someone. Amidst all of the chaos of the 21st century, someone had apparently taken the time to organize the "Northern Penobscot Tractor Pulling Association," not just the "Penobscot Tractor Pulling Association" version. In any case, NPTPA is a subset of the umbrella organization, the Maine Pulling Sled Owners Association. Their website says "Ear protection is STRONGLY RECOMMENDED for all spectators. They may be purchased at the pulling arena refreshment stand at a reasonable price."

The pull I saw later in Farmington confirmed that this was indeed a professional activity, as the tractor being pulled was different this time—called "The Dirt Dauber"—with a different logo. This was a puzzle, until I happened to run into a friend, Rick LePlant, who explained it all to me. I asked him if the tractor really had no other purpose in life than to be pulled by someone's pickup truck or even garden tractor.

"Oh, yeah," he said, "that's a special piece of equipment there," nodding at the tractor which had just finished being pulled, and was now being driven in reverse by its own engine. "You'll see some with different weights for different types of pulls, and that box on top there"—which I hadn't noticed before—"that's the mechanical drag. It moves forward to increase the weight as it's being pulled by the truck."

Other, non-competing pickup trucks were backed up to the edge of the pulling area in Farmington, people sitting in lawn chairs in the beds, huddling under blankets and with coolers and hot food close at hand. It wasn't long after the local high school's football game had ended, and it had that sort of feel to it, a football game, the stands filled with partisans, cheering on a pickup truck dubbed "Dirt Digger." The lights on the infield portion of the racetrack hummed, illuminating these roaring monsters, which gave the scene a nice apocalyptic feel.

The kind of things you see and hear at the Fair: At Clinton a man I've never met stops me and says, "See that fat blond over there? I saw her headed for me and I had to brace myself when she ran into me." I have no idea why he's telling me this, or why he didn't just step out of the way of the—admittedly—large blond woman. I also see a letter on display in the Clinton Historical Society building (actually more of a tent), from someone named George C. True, on Clinton Telegraph Company stationary, written during a winter in World War Two, to Mr. True's brother, which complains, "It is only 9,999 ½ below" and adds, "been stealing farmer's telephones—have got 4 so far."

At Windsor there is a booth that sells the chance to have your photograph taken with a python draped around your neck, and a display with "Kids! Free Movies!" over the door, meant to entice children inside, and which I think should be investigated by the Child Welfare Office, but which turns up at nearly every Fair and is showing a film on religion. And another that asks you to open three doors to answer the question, "Why Jesus died for you." The outdoor tables of items for sale, including belt buckles, blankets, nylon cowboy hats, Egyptian cotton sheets; T-shirts by the thousands (one reads, "If you aren't behind our troops, get in front of them"—the accompanying image is of soldiers in the background with rifles pointing at scruffy-looking citizens in front; another, which I see at several fairs reads, "Keep Staring—I Might Do a Trick." It's a little hard to puzzle out the message of that shirt.)

Clinton hosted a civil war encampment, the only one I see during my Fair odyssey. An exhibit at just about every Fair was a booth with a sign saying, "See What God Can't Do" above a row of three boxes. The point, of course, was to open each door and see nothing inside, the nothing that God can't do. At Farmington a woman plays religious songs, badly, on a scratchy violin at a church booth, and there is an outdoor table labeled "Prayer Station," attended by three people wearing red change bibs, and I can't put these together: are you really expected to stand and pray at the Prayer Station? And why would you need change to do so, and what is in the bibs if not change? It is a mystery that remains unsolved, as I didn't stop; no one else did either.

One day at Farmington there is a large man in a diaper wandering around. A big diaper, shoes and socks, a shirt, no pants; no explanation, no sign, just a diaper. Another day there is a man in a penguin suit, again for no apparent reason. I see a candidate for Congress, whose strident candidacy I don't support, at many of the Fairs. At Harmony he puts a juice box into a can clearly marked "recyclable cans/bottles" which confirms my non-vote for him. Republican booths tend to be more common than Democratic ones, although at the Blue Hill Fair, where the Ellsworth-American newspaper has set up a booth for people to have their picture taken with full-size cutouts of either Obama or McCain, more people have stood with Obama in mid-August than with McCain, even in this blue-collar part of the state. As I pass through one Fair parking lot I see a bumper sticker that catches my eye: "Reunite Gondwanaland!" it reads, and I think, Yes, Gondwanaland must be reunited! But then I wonder, What's Gondwanaland? It sounds vaguely familiar, somewhat African, but I realize I don't know what or where it is, so I can't entirely get behind the Reunite Gondwanaland campaign. Only later do

I remember it is the name for the southern continent that once included Australia, India, South America and Africa, before the continents separated 130 million years ago, more or less.

I witness line dancing being performed in a tent, observe the drowned clown game, a truck which holds a miniature house on the back that doubles as the "Peanut House," selling roasted nuts at most of the larger fairs; appreciate Golden-laced, Mottled, Buff, Brown Leghorn, and Ancona chickens, and watch a young 4-H'er using hair spray on her cow, then running a vacuum over its coat.

The outlier among Maine Fairs is the Common Ground Fair in Unity. How perfect to have Fairs in Harmony, and how appropriate that the "Common Ground" is in a place called Unity, especially as the Common Ground Fair is the hippie Fair, the alternative Maine Fair.

I have volunteered on Sunday at the Fair, to do . . . more or less anything. Lots of people volunteer at the Common Ground— you get in free by volunteering, but it is also in the spirit of the place, all of us pitching in for the good of the community. Plus I get a cool t-shirt that announces "Volunteer" in red on a bright yellow background.

It is a perfect fall day—it is now the 3rd Sunday of September, overlapping with the closing weekend of Farmington Fair, and it is, both by custom and calendar, fall. A good day to have a light sweater, except in the middle of the day in the middle of the road in the sun, where I am, preventing drivers from continuing on Crosby Brook Road, which has now been declared a one-way exit road by the Fair organizers. It is my job to man the barricades, and to direct people where to park and where the entrance for volunteers is. I can't help note all the Priuses and Honda Fit's coming and going; hardly a pickup truck in sight.

A woman drives up to my station in a junked up car and with

a stud driven all the way through the skin below her lower lip. The backseat is littered with maps and the debris of travel, and a dog; I give her good directions on how to get to Boston and she gives me the beaming thanks of a fellow traveler, as though we are united in the counterculture of the Fair. I feel as though I've misrepresented myself: Wait, I want to say, I'm a professor, I get a regular paycheck, I follow the stock market! But she's gone. Oh well, Godspeed.

Everyone I see around me is a hipster, the older folks who were at the volunteer's gate when I got there, the people streaming into the Fair from many angles. Inside, the Fair is strangely quiet; a connoisseur of Fairs will notice this right away: none of the accompanying calliope or bad old disco songs playing while the Ferris wheel turns. Well, mostly. There is an outdoor bowl, the amphitheater, where musicians perform, and they are amplified. But there are no rides—a Fair and no rides!?—unless you count hay rides and rides from the parking lot to the Fairgrounds via a long wagon with benches pulled by a tractor or a team of horses.

There is a whiff of Woodstock at the CGF—not the whiff of anything illegal burning, or of piles of garbage or people caked in mud—but these are clearly some of the descendants—intellectually, spiritually, politically—of that scene. The crowd here is the youngest of the Fairs, and there is more wool, fleece, sandals, beards, bare feet, dreadlocks than you could gather together in any other place in Maine if you tried, or at least not since Phish quit having concerts up north. There are still baseball caps, but most are traditional Red Sox caps (red "B" on blue background, the cap that is issued to all males in New England at birth) rather than farm product or motor parts supply hats. There are commercial vendors, too, but here they are advertising composting toilets, not ATVs. Yet this is truly the most statewide Fair: it is not a *County* Fair, not even one identified by place name, not Oxford or Cumberland or Springfield, but only the Common Ground.

Still, there is overlap with other Fairs: a poultry barn, like usual, a sheep dog demonstration, a lumber cutting demonstration, Italian sausage, the same lemonade stand that it is at <u>every</u> Fair (although here they are required to use honey, not sugar, in making the lemonade, the Fair Manager, Jim Ahearn, tells me), fried seafood, and thank God, I see a couple walking around eating French fries. But I also see a whole tent full of women weaving wool, as though practicing for a performance, tents for alternative lifestyles, schools of ecology, and, most revealing, tables set up for Democrats, the Socialist Party, Veterans for Peace, but no Republicans ("We've asked," Jim Ahearn says with a shrug).

Half the people arrive at the Fair by parking off of Route 220 and walking down hill through a pine forest, to arrive at the bowl where the Fair is held. People even ride their bikes from a central gathering spot in Unity to the Common Ground. This all contributes to the feeling that you're separating yourself from the normal world, that you are intentionally entering an alternative, when you settle gently on to the Common Ground.

One is tempted to say that the rides at all Fairs are the same, but this is not so. There are more midway companies (including Pak Enterprises, Smokey's Greater Shows, D&L Amusements, Larry Cushing Enterprises, Rockwell Amusements) than one would expect, and the names of the rides are themselves magic: Octopus, Round-up, Tempest, Aladdin, Super Slide, Sizzler, Gravitron, Mind Power, Cat House, Zippy (and also the Zipper), Haunted House, Lightning Bolt, Tiltawhirl, Thunder Bolt, Rope Ladder, 1001 Nachts ("Night," in German for some reason), Sea Dragon, Rock and Roll, Hammer, Typhoon, Flying Bob's, and for the kids, Jeep Safari, Super Slide, Churning Around, (miniature) Ferris Wheel, Dragon, Dizzy Dragons (distinct from regular dragons), Aladdin, Train Station, Bumper Cars, and so on.

On a rainy night at the Cumberland County Fair, there is one lonely child riding on the Rock and Roll. Music blared and the ride raced around—one of those that undulated up and down on a set track—but he didn't seem to be either rocking or rolling.

There are only two types who ride the rides: small children on the miniature rides and merry-go-round, and possees of teenagers who descend in packs on the adult rides, especially the wilder ones. Oh, I suppose there is a third group, too: Older people, like me, who take the Ferris Wheel into the sky on a clear night with a huge autumn moon in sight, which seems to happen every year at the Farmington Fair. Be at Farmington late enough in the evening, and the moon will eventually come to the left hand side of the Ferris Wheel—which is always stationed on a northwest-southeast axis—having worked its way around from behind you; better if the big wheel were arranged so that as you rose you faced the full moon, but it is good enough to have it this way, lifting into the soft sky, feeling as though you are approaching the moon, rising to its level. Best of all if you get stuck at the top of the wheel while someone is let out at the bottom, and you and the moon and your loved one are alone in the Farmington heavens.

But otherwise the rides are for screaming, or for quiet terror, in the case of the little ones. At Windsor I watched kids hold tight to toy motorcycles, their faces an exquisite combination of intensity, fear, joy. There is no pleasure to be had from riding with a herd of teenagers, but watching your own child, wide-eyed, move slowly around on the merry-go-round, calliope-like sounds pumping from the sound system, is one of the certain joys of parenthood.

One should witness a pig scramble before one dies. It is a singular event, combining small kids, smaller pigs, and a bizarre race.

I saw my first and only scramble at the Cumberland Fair, though several Fairs have them. Cumberland is a bit north of Portland, and the Fair is out in the country, between West Cumberland and Cumberland Center. In other words, nowhere, occupying its own dimension in the universe, known as, "Fairground."

I went there on a very wet Friday night in late September. It wasn't the best time to see a Fair, but it was the only time I had free, and the Fair was closing at the end of the weekend. It was pitch black when I arrived, and only a few people—under umbrellas or hanging onto plastic sheets spread out to cover three at once, like jellyfish floating in this sea of rain—moved about. Most of the food stalls had closed, including Fat Guy's Famous Sausage and Steak, Big Al's Fries, and Southern Style BBQ.

The scramble was held in the small 4-H arena, not far from the muddy entrance to the Fair. I was drawn to the contest by the high-pitched sound of pigs squealing in terror. A full boar roar. Apparently one had been picked up, and pigs, apparently, do not like to be picked up. I took a seat in the grandstand along with a smattering of others, mostly parents of contestants or people trying to keep out of the rain. An announcer called for the first group of kids to get ready, which meant a handful of children of middle-school age came out with the pigs, either carrying them in full squeal, or herding them along, until the pigs were forced into their own chutes in a weird wooden box that had a front gate on it. Then smaller kids, third-graders, the pigs' owners, came up and gave his or her pig a bite of some treat—popular items were turkey dogs, granola bar, and hot dog—but only a bite, holding on to the rest of it so that the pig would want to race to that same taste when the contest began. Then the kids hustled down to the far end of the arena, and took seats in a row against the far wall, with some distance between one another. The kids and their pigs were introduced (I took note of the fact one pig was named "Harper," same as my daughter, which I tell her later; she is not amused) and at the announcer's call, the gate was lifted on the holding stand, and the little pigs trotted out.

It wasn't exactly a race, unless one considers aimless wandering in several directions a "race." The pigs went forward out of the holding stand, then maybe turned around, or went to the left or right. Gradually they became aware of something worthwhile straight ahead and would start moving that direction, and at some point they might have picked up the smell of the remainder of the snack given to them before. The beloved pig owner didn't seem to be much of an attraction, as the pigs only vaguely headed towards the proper chair, while the kids screamed their names and the families in the stands urged them on. The kids weren't allowed to leave their chairs, and could only stretch out, waving the treat towards the oblivious pig. When the kid could touch the pig the race was over for that pig and kid; in this case, pig #6 in a red vest came in first. The last team of kid-and-pig to conjoin were always far behind the others, which had elements of both pathos and comedy about it.

One teenage girl in the stands scoffed at the inability of the teenagers to corral the pigs for the race. Her father leaned over and asked, "Ever tried to catch a pig?" rhetorically. It struck me this was exactly the function of the Fair, to remind us of what we don't know, what we've lost touch with, what has disappeared between one generation and another: the ability to successfully grab a pig.

After wandering around the rainy, dark Fair—is there anything more gloomy than a dripping, funereal, sparsely attended Fair with few rides running and most of the food stalls closed and a pretty decent country band, the Don Campbell Band, who deserved better, playing in a cavernous metal shed in front of 19 people?— I discovered another treasure in a far corner of the Fairgrounds. This treasure wasn't hard to find, as all of the people who weren't at the rest of the Fair were here, and the space was filled with light. It was the pulling arena, packed to the rafters with witnesses, there to see the International Pulling Contest, pitting Canada against the United States of America. It was the only international pulling contest to be held in Maine, in New England; for all I knew, in the world.

I had stumbled on an epic event, medieval combat. Teams of huge horses, buckled and strapped into leather and metal, like some sort of warrior tribe caparasoned for battle, stamped their huge hoofs, and big men stood in front of or beside them, one large hand on the flanks of the animal or its straps.

I squeezed into a spot along the fence, since there were no places to be had in the stands. After some struggles to get the horses into the right spots—all backed into places along the fence where I stood so the group of us were facing their back ends—the ring announcer began introducing the teams and their "drivers"—the accepted term for what they do. There were three teams from Nova Scotia, three from Maine. Elaborate introductions were given, with background, history, successes, and sometimes an amusing tag line tossed in, obviously composed by the driver himself.

The event began, oddly, with a prayer. The minister or prayer-giver asks for a "safe pull" and it occurs to me to wonder whose safety we're after here, the drivers or the horses, or both? Following prayers came national anthems; apparently no ceremonial aspect was to be overlooked. A recording played over the loudspeaker, first "O Canada" then "The Star Spangled Banner." Around the stands I saw people mouthing words to the anthems, although there seemed to be some disagreement about the lyrics, as different people mouthed different words. Right at "the bombs streaming in air" one horse let loose with a tremendous stream of urine, and people around me glanced sideways at one another, knowing they'd better not laugh.

Finally we get to the pull. There are an infinite number of pulling events, it seems, some involving old time skills like twitching logs (*aka*, pulling logs out of the woods), or pulling logs through an obstacle course, but tonight's pulling affair is sheer muscle and strength. The horse team (always two) is backed up to the sled they are to pull and the heavy wooden harness is slipped over a pin on the front of the sled. The sleds themselves are designed for just this purpose, as with the tractor pull monstrosity. They have two runners, are about six feet long, and carry pads of cement to test the horses' strength. Different fairs use different-weight cement pads, but here at Cumberland the pads were 400 pounds each, stacked on top of one another. A tractor is used to lift the blocks on and off the sled, and to pull the sled back after the end of each pull.

The first puller is a dark-eyed man from Lincoln. He is very intense, almost mean, as he works with his horses, but when he is done with the pull, when they've pulled all they can pull, he laughs and pats them on the flank. Then Junior Blanchard from Kingdom, Maine. Junior wears a cowboy hat, jeans, cowboy boots, and an untucked flannel shirt. His horses make a nice pull, going all the way to the end of the arena. The second driver is Josh Daniels from Nova Scotia. His team pulls nine thousand pounds; four and a half tons sounds like a lot to pull. The team fails at ninety-four hundred pounds, and I don't blame them.

It is the failures that are most interesting about the pulls. The horses aren't the only ones pulling; you can feel the crowd pulling as well, tensing with the animals as they strain. I can't tell for sure, but it looks as though the horses love to pull. They paw the ground before the pull, as though readying themselves; one rears up on its hind legs, so anxious is he to get going. And when the command comes—and there is no telling when it will come, as the drivers seem to pick a magic moment out of the air, when their horses are just right, when the conditions are perfect, when the horses have recovered from the last effort but aren't wasting energy being anxious; hard to tell what makes the right moment but something does—and the horses lurch forward, the chains snapping, their belts and harnesses cracking against their flanks, and the horse's forelegs bend backwards with the strain of pulling, and they seem so determined to inch that sled a bit further forward, and you in your seat strain forward a little with them.

To be successful, the team must pull the weighted sled at least thirty-six inches. A metal stand tied to the back of the sled by a thirty-six inch length of rope is placed right behind the sled to begin, then if the sled is pulled that far and the stand topples over, the arena announcer monotones "All the way." At first I didn't understand the refrain, as it isn't said with any particular enthusiasm or triumph, but merely descriptively: but the refrain refers to the fact the team has made it "all the way" it needs to go. One team, as dedicated as any other, failed at 34-and-a-half inches, instead of 36. The crowd groaned; it seemed important to make that final inch and a half, but alas, it was not to be.

Ultimately the Maple Leaf triumphed over the Stars and Stripes, as Nova Scotia bested Maine. You could tell this was going to be the case from the outset, as the horses from Nova Scotia were huge, as though from another country, a country that requires huge horses in order to survive.

Before I abandoned Cumberland to the dismal night, I took in some sheltering sheds: One building was devoted to pigs, another to rabbits. This was another surprise about Fairs, that rabbits would be so important to so many (Oxford, Fryeburg, Farmington, and others). A great variety of rabbits, ones I'd never heard of, strange looking ones: Fuzzy Lop, French Angora, Britannia Petite, Harlequin, Himalayan, Jersey Wooly, and Mini Rex. And then, in one of the odd touches that seem to abound at Fairs, "Lucky Rabbit Feet" being sold in the building for $2.50 a pop. Either I'm missing something important and valuable about combining live rabbits with dead rabbit parts, or someone has no feel for irony.

Somehow it had become standard procedure for hand washing stations to be on all the doorways to the animal exhibit halls, whether bovine, ursine or poultry. Fred Lunt said there was no rule about this, just that the Fairs were working with the Department of Health and Human Services to prevent *e coli* outbreaks from occurring. The idea appears to be that one will be tempted to touch the cow, sheep, lamb, chicken, and in this Age of Disease, one will want to hurriedly wipe off that residue. This leaves aside the issue of how the owners survive, since they touch the animals constantly.

As for the pigs, I made the obligatory tour through their quarters—one feels obliged to be a witness at the Fair, to attend to all things displayed and laid out for one's attention, so I'll wander through any exhibit, just to acknowledge what is there. I saw "Jeff" a Grand Champion pig, born on February 29, 2008 (a Leap Year pig!); on September 26th of that same year he is huge. Another pig, "Ellsbury," named after the Red Sox centerfielder no doubt, took a rather embarrassing 6th place in a contest. He senses my contempt and snorts derisively as I walk past. I stop and realize I don't know what it's like to catch a pig, or what a pig's snout feels like, so I reach over and give his bristly snout a stroke. He doesn't mind, no one yells at me, and I don't insult Ellsbury by washing my hands afterward; after all, I reason, it was only a finger. And now I know what a pig's snout feels like, which I wouldn't have known if I hadn't come to the Fair.

Later, in January, I attend the Annual Meeting of the Maine Association of Agricultural Fairs in Portland, at the Holiday Inn on Spring Street. There are sessions on "The Value of Good Entertainment at Your Fair" and "Off Season Activities for Fairs" and the "Pulling Superintendent's Meeting." Fred Lunt is much in demand at this gathering, and I see more suspenders in one day than I've seen collectively in decades. I hear a man return a greeting with a "yessuh" that is the most perfect example of that classic Maine phrase I have ever heard.

I sit in on a couple of sessions, including the Livestock Superintendents and Exhibitors Meeting, run by a man named Curtis who has what I think of as a great country face and who is passionate about the virtues of the animal exhibits at a Fair. "People come to the Fairs for the animals. Surveys show this," says Curtis. "But there aren't as many exhibits as in the past—the young people don't get involved," though another person in attendance points out that 4-H participation has increased recently. Various people speak on the successes they've had with their animal exhibits, and the meeting teeters between bleak prospects for the future and current triumphs.

At the Draft Horse & Ox Association meeting controversy erupts. After a roll call of all of the Fairs—only a few don't have a representative—in which they briefly report on changes (Blue Hill notes that they are getting rid of the twenty-one hundred pound class, and "tweaking on the horse pulling," but not sure just how yet), the subject turns to animal testing. One can tell by the shifting in the hall and the postures that this is a sore topic, and that people are ready for a fight. A big man, Seth Bradstreet, the Commissioner of Agriculture, stands up and explains the need for animal testing, and the state veterinarian, Dr. Hoenig, answers questions. Seth claims that "we're trying to help you have a good pull, so that everyone knows the animals are all clean, and we're trying to protect the animals." Another leader of the meeting says "we're trying to keep one step ahead of the animal activists." I had no idea this was an issue, so I ask Fred about it, and he says "it's not a problem, but we don't want it to become one. We've got two animal welfare organizations on the pulling board, helping us keep the pulls safe and humane."

They are discussing the doping of the animals, the horses and oxen and steers. Just as with human athletes, there apparently is a temptation to chemically enhance the animals used in these pulling contests. Since the maximum purse for a pulling contest in Maine is about $75, it's hard to see why one would bother.

Seth goes over the punishments: two year suspension for the puller, one year for the animal. A list has already been started that contains the names of those whose animals have tested positive. A man from Blue Hill speaks up, barely able to contain his outrage. "I'm the one who they said got caught with cocaine in my animal." He pauses. "I've never seen cocaine in my life," he adds, firmly, and looking at him, it is hard to imagine that he ever has. "How can I protect my animal from being tainted?" he appeals. All around the big meeting room, people shake their heads in agreement.

Seth repeats that they will work with the owners to try and avoid mistakes. Someone gets mad at Fred about the testing program, and a back and forth bantering unfolds. I head for lunch.

The Farmington Fair is not a Fair so much as it is a meteorological marvel. Locals know to plan for Fair week. "The best week for painting houses is Fair Week," I've been told, and indeed with few exceptions the week of the Farmington Fair is cool, clear, windless, and dry. From the start of Fair Week, in flip flops, to the end, in a sweatshirt or fleece, the weather in this mid-September stretch is the best Maine has to offer. And somehow there is always a full moon during Fair Week—I don't know how this can be, but it is.

On Wednesday of Fair Week in 2008, the magically-annual full moon rose on the far side of the race track, so that those of us in the grandstand by the race track had a superb view of it, lifting just above the band shell where the Franklin County Fiddlers, a local high school fiddling group, played. Off on the north side of the race track, in the pulling arena, transformed this night into a wrestling ring, we could hear the shouts and the announcer's roar, but here in the grandstand, we were being civilized by the sounds of bluegrass, Cajun music, by the sound of these rural Mainers playing complicated fiddle tunes. All night long that impossibly round moon dominated the Fair, as though a cheesy paper cutout had been added to the Fair, to make it, Fair.

I went to Farmington Fair every day of Fair Week, from the Sunday when it opened to the Sunday when it closed. I made it my task to attend those things I'd never attended before. First the pulling arena, "dedicated to the Hall Family" as the sign says on the inside of the barn, above the "pulling office." Here I saw a vast array of pulls, more than twenty contests. There were the usual pulling-of-heavy-objects-by-huge-farm animals (steer, oxen, or horse), although nothing so dramatic as the Cumberland Fair International Competition. Some of the pulls were "Open to the World" which sounded like Farmington, Maine was ready to take on the entire planet when it came to horse pulling.

My favorite was the twitching obstacle course, which involved pairs of oxen pulling a log around and between cones set in a sort of figure-eight pattern. One contestant, a toddling older man named Jesse Pierce, led two oxen that towered over him as he hobbled around the course, as though they were loyal dogs, desperate to stay close to their master. One trotted so close behind it nearly trampled him.

A series of hand gestures and shouts and slaps with a thin stick were the ways driver and beast communicated, impossible to decipher by a layman, except that you could tell that sometimes fear was involved, other times love. Jesse led his oxen around in smart order, speaking sharply if they headed out of line but that was all. Another driver, during a pulling contest, when his team had paused between pulls, would suddenly run at them, roaring and waving his arms, to get them moving. He was a big man, tall and powerful, and it was a little disturbing to see this assault on his team, but no one else seemed particularly disturbed, though Fred Lunt did mutter about such tactics, saying

"We don't want to see the animals work under fear. Usually," he added, "the animals are in the pulling because they've been trained to do it and conditioned for it, and they have a relationship with the teamster so that they do it because the teamster wants them to, because it pleases him."

When I asked a teamster at the Friday night pull what else he used his horses for, he mistook my question for an animal rights challenge and simmered: "If these horses weren't doing this they'd be in Japan, on someone's plate. If you see a horse doing this you should be damn glad they're doing it," and stomped away.

One day I headed indoors, to the long, tall halls of the Franklin County Agricultural Exhibit hall, a building whose outside proclaims that the Farmington Fair started in 1840. It is two-story building of many purposes; attached to one end, just outside the official exhibition hall, is a low building that holds the Elks Lodge cafe. On the other end, inside the hall itself, is another small café carved out of one corner, where a Methodist Church always supplies food, usually good, healthy basic food, like soups and pies. I never eat there. Halfway on the first level is one of the entrances to the Fair, so that when you enter you are smack in the middle of canning jars and pumpkins and grange exhibits and crafts made of wood.

I always walk these floors when I come to the Fair. The wide, wooden floors are soothing, and there are few things more charming than all of these objects and products that value small town and rural life. I usually just wander, see if there is anyone I know represented in the displays; this time I took note of Arlene Welch's "Muffins (3)" which got a 1st Premium ribbon. Aileen Kennedy's basket took a second. One of the popular categories for crafts was "Holiday and Seasonal other than Christmas." "Witchy-Washy" came in 1st in this category, made by Linda Allen. Another category is "Best Article—Tole Art." First place went to Alberta Currier of New Sharon, for a painted tree fungus;

at least that's what I thought it was. Other categories were "My Pet" and "My Family" in photography. There were dill pickles that took a second, green beans that took first, bread and butter sliced pickles, dill spears, sour mustard, celery pickles, cucumber cinnamon.

I saw exhibits by Grange#202 from Strong, with its hand-painted circular saw blades, hand-sewn pillow cases, colorful wooden stools, beaded Indian costumes. I saw Italian Green Tomatoes: Wilda McDaniel of Fayette took a 1st Premium for a half-dozen Italian Green Tomatoes (Division 3, Class 49). The Chesterville Grange, #20, also took a 1st Premium for their display, and another category was "Charity, Love, Home, Faith." There were quilts, other sewn items, and Best Art Woodcraft, Handmade (Division 4, Class 72). Third place went to a boat with a stick for a mast and a piece of pink rag as the sail. I saw Tall Top Early Wonder beets, and prize winning eggs. The eggs stopped me short: how do you judge an egg?

At the end of Fair week I journeyed again to the race track, but this time to bet on a race. As usual, the end of the week had become brisk, as Farmington Fair begins in summer and ends in fall. The crowd, all middle-aged or older, in mid-day was clothed in hooded sweatshirts and fleece jackets that had scenes of hunting life on them, or some with the names of vacation destinations—Puerto Vallarta, Disneyworld—or cruise ships. Everyone was gathered in the sunlight between the betting office and the grandstand, to suck up a bit of the sun's heat, and avoid the cool shadows in the grandstand itself.

I strode up to the betting office window and confidently placed my bet, having looked over the odds announced on the electronic scoreboard on the inside of the track. I put two dollars down on horse #14, but there was no horse #14; I'd mistaken the odds (14-1) for the horse's number. The clerk gently, only slightly contemptuously, corrected me and we got the money played properly.

The race begins and the announcer's incomprehensible chatter accompanies the horses around the bends. Can't make out a word until he hits on a name, like "Blue Bell," that is familiar. "Unbridled Enthusiasm" has too many syllables to be heard clearly. The horses prance in the strange mincing steps that are required when a horse is attached to a cart, a rather spindly cart upon which the driver nearly reclines. A man in a camo hat in front of me says to the woman he's with, "Want to see a horse die?" She looks nervously at him. "Bet on it," he says, "that'll kill it for sure." He laughs. My horse loses, badly.

No one claps, no one curses, they only take out their Racing Programs and look to the next race, except for the few who head over to the "winning" window to get paid for their astute betting. Somehow this racing and gambling doesn't seem part of the Fair experience—perhaps part of that "frivolous and corrupt" trend the Grangers from the century-before-last complained of—but in the sunshine on a mild day, it's not a bad way to pass an hour or two. It's nice to see the horses running, pulling their riders in the strange carts they ride in. The horses don't seem overtaxed, no one seems to be in any danger of breaking anything, and the betting is restrained.

The 4-H show on Friday is not well-advertised, but the barn where it is to take place is packed. I hadn't planned on coming, but was in the barn area when it began and was attracted by the crowd, by the sense of something unfolding that I should witness. A small area was fenced off at one end of the barn, and a man using an incredibly scratchy sound system was attempting to get things started. People were seated on a small set of bleachers on one side, everywhere else people stood, peering over each other's shoulders. A narrow walkway was cleared from a holding area to the showing pen, and once we got started, pretty teenage girls led their lambs out into the ring.

The first girl led her lamb out and then pulled up on its neck from behind, so that its head pointed skyward. This was some sort of displaying strategy, but I couldn't tell to what purpose. It looked a little unnatural, a little uncomfortable for the animal, but knowing nothing, I assumed it was part of the 4-H training the girls had received.

Then the man with the scratchy microphone began calling for bids, and I looked more closely at the flyer tacked on the barn wall: "4-H Show and Sale," it read. I'd not noticed the "sale" part. I found this mildly disturbing, as I watched these pretty, blond teenagers, who had lovingly raised these animals, hold them out for purchase and instant slaughter; the lambs and hogs would be packaged meat by the end of the day. I saw a man I've known for years, an insurance salesman, bid on a steer, winning it at two dollars per pound. I asked him later if that was a good price. Beaming, he said, "Oh God, no. I buy just to support the 4-H. I give most of the meat away."

I looked for some sign of discomfort in the girls, some traces of attachment, of the natural emotion that might accompany the surrendering of a companion, but there was none, at least none that I was allowed to see. From the outside, where I stood, it seemed cruel for them to sell their pets, especially for slaughter—there was something of the slave auction to the event, where to those on the inside there isn't anything at all unusual about the ethics of such an activity, while those outside of that world might find it appalling. I knew I was too far outside the 4-H sale to judge, and I also know that if animals are going to be raised and slaughtered, then an event such as the 4-H show and sale shouldn't be surprising.

There are few contrasts more startling than that between a Fair in full swing and a Fair in the morning or early afternoon. At those times the Fair is a contemplative, quiet place, almost like a farm or a barnyard. Older fair-goers lean quietly against a barn, having a cup of coffee and blueberry muffins offered by the History Museum, chatting with neighbors, or attending to the animals, or discussing the exhibits in the historical museum or the craft barns. There is no music playing, no generators roaring, as the rides have fallen silent and the food stalls have just begun to open. It is so quiet I can hear a man in the History Museum say "That's what Noah said—always be prepared," which I can't decide is a joke or an old saying or an original observation.

I saw both Litchfield ("Everything a Fair Should Be," read a sign on the Town Hall) and Oxford Fairs in this sleepy condition. Oxford had an outhouse on display, labeled "Genuine Maine Outhouse," Litchfield showed off antique cars. Both had bathroom attendants who cleaned and stocked the bathrooms for tips. Oxford provided deep-fried whoopee pies, which I never saw anywhere else, as well as chicken fingers and fried pork wings, a description which is a puzzle, an unlikely combination: pork + wings.

And then, finally, the end of the season came, as it must, as it does every year, at Fryeburg. No one calls it "the Fryeburg Fair"—it is only "Fryeburg," as in "Going to Fryeburg this year?"

Driving to this distant Fair in the extreme western and southern part of the state late in a national election year, I am dazzled both by the colors of the trees, which are at their most robust, but also by the competition they get from the hundreds of candidate signs, which, on Route 140 and Route 117 and Route 118 and 5, through East Sumner and Jim Hill and Pumpkin Valley, are a riot of colors, clustered at every stop sign and junction, a burst of color below, the trees a different burst above. Winding my way through the little towns on the tiny roads, is like traveling through a river of colors. I get to pass through anonymous little towns like East Stoneham, with its welcome sign that says "A little town overflowing with traditions."

Fryeburg is the giant of and the exclamation point to the season. The place is vast, so vast it even has tunnels underneath the race track to allow for the flow of people back and forth from one part of the Fair to another. The aisles for food and games are tight, and tall, with facades stretching up high, and walking this alley feels most like being in a medieval city—dirt and sawdust beneath you, a slightly crazed jumble of desperate and rowdy minstrels hounding you from all sides.

Fryeburg has the biggest racetrack and grandstand, the largest number of animal barns and exhibition halls, the most rides, food, games, and the only marching band I've seen during Fair season, marching in a polyglot parade on the race track on the second to last day of the 2008 Fair season. The parade involves cows, oxen, sheep, a brass band pulled on a trailer, the marching band, pulling teams; pairs of oxen join the parade, including two sets led by two middle-aged twin sisters with similarly curly white hair, and it goes on and on, past the grandstand as an announcer introduces each, while new members of the parade pull into line from outside the track or from the grass infield.

Having seen tractor pulls, demolition derbies, horse and oxen pulls; having seen animal auctions and moldy tomatoes and desiccating green beans, and stroked the nose of a hog and witnessed the poultry, I finally engage with cows at Fryeburg. On this last weekend the judging is over, and navigating through the stalls I see ribbon after ribbon. One winner is standing out front of a barn, being hosed off. A crowd gathers around and the owners patiently pose for picture after picture with little kids who want to stand next to, but not too close to, this enormous being, as though doing so is a kind of dare.

They take their animals seriously at Fryeburg. The sign on a barn reads "If you don't own them, leave them alone." On another barn the sign is "Absolutely no manure this end of barn," which conjures an unpleasant picture of what the other end will look like.

I lose track of how many barns there are as I wander through them. Each of the cows in one barn has its name displayed on a sign in its stall. Nitro, Babe, Maple, Tom, Fred, Jake, Jim, Joe, Ben, Buck, Red, Rusty, Zeus, Hercules, Star, Stripe, Hank, Willie, Fred, Milo, Barnie, are all in residence today. It appears one or two syllables is the preferred limit, except for the mouthful of "Hercules."

Why do so many farmers bring their animals here; what's in it for them? I stop to ask a man tending to his cow. Do you get any money if you win? "Oh sure," he says, "there's a prize for first, second and third, ten in all I think. Not much, maybe fifty bucks if you win. Some people do it just as a hobby, but some guys here will sell their cows or steers after the Fair, and the better they place, the more money they'll get for them."

There are a lot of cows and oxen and steer. Someone tells me there are 330 cows showing at the Fair this year. They can't <u>all</u> be placing first, second, or third or even tenth. What about the others, I ask. "Oh, some guys'll use them in the woods, alright, and some guys, if they [meaning the cows] don't show, they'll beef 'em." I'm stumped by "beef 'em" but don't ask for an explanation, not wanting to appear ignorant about this technical term, but it dawns on me later: "beef 'em" means to turn them into beef, of course. It seems like an unfitting end for these nurtured beasts, but with the smell of hamburgers drifting over the Fair, along with lamb and chicken and fish, it is hard to argue with the order of things. The Fair deals in both ends of life, acknowledges both. I am reminded of that cow back in Blue Hill, a month ago, giving birth with a crowd of witnesses, and the 4-H sale in Farmington, and the nonchalant auctioning of animals that have been raised to be slaughtered. The Fair is not the place to ponder animal rights or vegetarianism.

Fryeburg is <u>crowded</u>, packed, the aisles filled with people. One has to jostle and step strategically in order to move along, and the families with strollers make slow headway in the crowds.

Everything is here at Fryeburg, all the rides, all the games, all the farm animal contests and museums and old school houses and maple sugaring display and pig contests and race tracks and bad Fair food. I see a hay press in the museum, something I've never seen before, eat awful fried haddock and pay $3.75 for a tiny bag of maple-flavored kettle corn. I see a teenager wearing a t-shirt that says "You see me" in the front and "Hi Hater" on the back, which makes absolutely no sense; another set of teenage girls with matching "Marijuana" ball caps on. I watch a pig-judging contest, where the announcer is an expert on types of pigs, including the Hampshire variety that is being shown, along with a Black hog, which, as he says, "is a bacon hog," raising the question of which hogs aren't? "Very few in this country," he says, referring to the Black, adding, "it has fallen behind in genetic selection." A man next to me says "Look at the size of that monstrosity," which sounds unkind, given the pig's failings in the genetic selection department.

One of the carneys manning the Haunted House ride bangs on the sheet metal front to scare the people riding in carts inside; he knows just when to do it, just when they will be passing that spot, and is adding his special touch to the experience. Nice to see someone take pleasure in his work. I play three games of Skeeball, maxing out at 90 points. I thought I needed only 60 points to win a treasure, but it turns out I read it wrong—it is "160" not 60, so once again I fail to secure a stuffed animal at a Fair. After nearly a dozen Fairs, I don't bring home a single doll.

Fryeburg feels as though it has absorbed every other Fair of the summer—it has the elements of them all, it combines them all. It is a planet, exerting gravitational force, pulling in people from all over northern New England, even people who will camp for the week in the parking lot across Route 5 from the Fairgrounds.

I have done my research, I have had my Fair, I am ready to draw my conclusions; specifically, about the mystery of the one thing that unites all Fairs, that a Fair apparently cannot do without. The cheap answer would be that they all had exhibitions, animals, rides, but I was looking for something more specific, some certain, fixed, identifiable, single thing. And at last I found it, after dismissing one possibility then another, until only one object was left. That thing all Fairs had, without exception, that Harmony offered and Oxford provided, and that probably is available at every Fair, everywhere, in every universe and alternate universe, was a modest thing, but apparently crucial to the Fair experience, and that thing was . . .

Fried dough. Every Fair had fried dough; every single one. They might all have had onion rings, too, or cotton candy, but I'm absolutely sure of the fried dough. Because I'd never had fried dough before; the mere concept was too troubling. Why on earth would I want to eat dough that had been fried? I had always avoided it, even while consuming falafel, hot dogs, hamburgers, two bites of kielbasa, onion rings, fried haddock, gyros, candy apples and other things that ordinarily would never pass my lips.

So on the last half hour of my last day on nearly the last day of the last Fair of the season, I stepped up to a fried dough stand and placed my order. The woman inside the trailer, elevated above me, smiled wryly, as though she was in on the fact that this was my first time. "One dough," I said, as though I were an expert, a veteran.

"What kind?" she said.

Kinds? There are kinds of fried dough? I looked more closely at the menu on the trailer. Apparently I could have dough with cinnamon, with maple syrup, with powdered sugar, with stewed apples.

I took the powdered sugar option, figuring this was closest to the true essence of fried dough. Soon the woman handed me my dough, a big flat cylinder of hot dough, glistening from the fryer. I spooned some powdered sugar on to it and ate.

And discovered a doughnut. Fried dough is a big, flat doughnut, that's all. Like so many other things at the Fair, fried dough is not quite what it seems—it is neither exotic nor pedestrian, neither ordinary nor unusual.

You are a visitor to a foreign country while at a Fair. It is a country that vaguely resembles the one you are a citizen of, but that you had forgotten existed. You see traces of the country you know, but they are distant and hazy, as though you are looking through an old window whose panes have sagged. And then you realize it is the window itself you have been looking at, it is the sagging panes that caught your eye, and that, that is the country of the Fair.

This is what I found at the Fair: a real place, but not the real place you think at first it is. It is not quite false, yet not quite real. Cows that are raised to be displayed, pulling contests for horses and oxen that never pull anything else, crafts and vegetables that aren't used or consumed, only displayed. This doesn't make them false, only not quite the cows you expect, not the hard-working pulling beasts who are brought out to strut their stuff, not the knitted objects that are used in the home, not the food you will eat.

But you accept that, because someday you might own a cow, or need to knit something, or wonder how maple syrup is made or what an old schoolhouse in Maine looked like or what kind of tools they used on farms back then or what it takes to be a First Prize Tomato. Maybe you'll have a craving for a blooming onion, or a desire to see a pig, a horse straining to pull cement blocks, kids on a merry-go-round, the hurdy-gurdy man, cars smashing backwards into each other, or want to try out the stuffed-toy games you know you'll fail at, or eat the fried thing you never would otherwise eat, or find out the nothing that God can't do, or watch the couples and families stroll along absorbed in their own private Fair, and in the air feel fall ending and see the full moon which is always, always, there.

I ate the fried dough, knowing it was a doughnut; it was hot and sweet, and it was good.

Graduating

(2009)

The auditorium at the high school in Jackman, Maine was also a gym, the kind of gym where, if you went in too hard for a lay-up, you were likely to mash your face on the front of the performance stage, or, at the other end, fall through the serving area into the kitchen. It was sweltering inside, for early June, and I may have been the only person wearing a sport coat.

I was there as the commencement speaker for the high school graduation ceremony of Forest Hills High School, held to honor the tiny class of eleven. I was an unlikely commencement speaker. I'd never done one before and had no relation to the High School, or to Jackman for that matter, except for being there once, years before, flying in with a Maine Game Warden pilot who landed on Wood Pond and taxied up to a lawn near a café where we ate lunch. I didn't notice the café as I drove into town that afternoon, distracted by the impressive views to be had in all directions as one approaches the Moose River Valley in which Jackman rests.

I had been invited to speak by a former student, now an English teacher at Forest Hills, and, given the novelty of the invitation, couldn't refuse. My job, as with most commencement speakers, was to say something meaningful, but not take too long about it. I thought I knew what I would say as soon as I agreed to give the talk. I wrote a couple of drafts, tinkered a bit, read it out loud once or twice, and was set.

There had been many pieces to the program by the time my turn came—a song sung by a local mother; a slide show covering the lives of the graduating seniors; flowers delivered by the seniors to family members in the audience; Pomp and Circumstance played on a rickety old piano; introductions of each of the seniors; the Class President's greeting; the valedictorian's speech, done partly in French, in homage to Quebec next door.

Then me. I mounted the wooden steps to the stage, told the seniors closest to the podium in a stage whisper that I'd be quick, which got a grateful smile, then launched in.

I said that I would be briefer and less profound than Ralph Waldo Emerson in his famous Divinity School Address, and longer and less profound than Lincoln at Gettysburg; told them I wasn't going to offer any advice, as they were now graduates, the ones who knew things the rest of us didn't know, or had now forgotten, and besides, "one shouldn't take advice from strangers," and then I introduced my theme: "I want to tell you how lucky you are to be graduates of Forest Hills High School in Jackman, Maine, hard by the Quebec border," and, "you are the fortunate few precisely because you are here, in Jackman. Eighty percent of Americans now live in what are defined as urban or suburban environments, where, if they're lucky, they have an eighth of an acre of land with a house on it—you have space here. Most Americans spend about 25 minutes a day commuting to work, 100 hours per year, in traffic; if you drive 25 minutes a day to school, I'm guessing it isn't in traffic; Most Americans don't know their neighbors; you do. And from my point of view, the most important reason why you're lucky is that every day you have a fairly immediate experience with the natural world; most Americans don't."

I had hit my stride, I was on my way home, I was feeling good about the message I was delivering. I assured them they should be proud of being from a small town, that they were lucky in all sorts of quirky ways to be different from the rest of 21st century

America. And then it dawned on me: they probably knew this. It might never have occurred to them to doubt that they were lucky, or to be ashamed of being from the small town of Jackman ("the Switzerland of Maine"); they didn't need to be told they were unusual and to be envied, even in a stuffy auditorium *cum* gym.

It was an act of hubris, a remnant of the assumptions I brought to Maine with me from urban California years ago. I got halfway through my speech and began to sweat—not just from the suffocating room—realizing it was all wrong, I'd written the wrong speech, my assurances to the graduates about their uniqueness, unneeded.

Fortunately, the eleven forgave me. I left Jackman with a brand-new Forest Hills "Tigers" ball cap, a tie, and a gift certificate for a steak dinner in town, and a reminder that rural living doesn't require excuses, or apologies, or defenses. At least I'd been right about one thing: they did possess knowledge I'd forgotten, or not yet learned.

About the Author

Michael D. Burke is the author of *The Same River Twice: A Boatman's Journey Home*, and of essays and articles in *Down East*, *The New York Times*, *Boston Globe*, *Yankee*, *Islands*, *Maine Décor* and the *Times* of South Africa. For over 35 years he was a whitewater and wilderness river guide in Idaho, Oregon, California and Alaska, with other descents in Mexico and British Columbia. He is Professor Emeritus of Creative Writing and English at Colby College in Maine, where he was Director of the Creative Writing program from 2017 to 2022.

He lives in Wilton, Maine with his wife, the writer Patricia O'Donnell. They have three grown children.